AF342347

GANDHI
the Eternal Youth

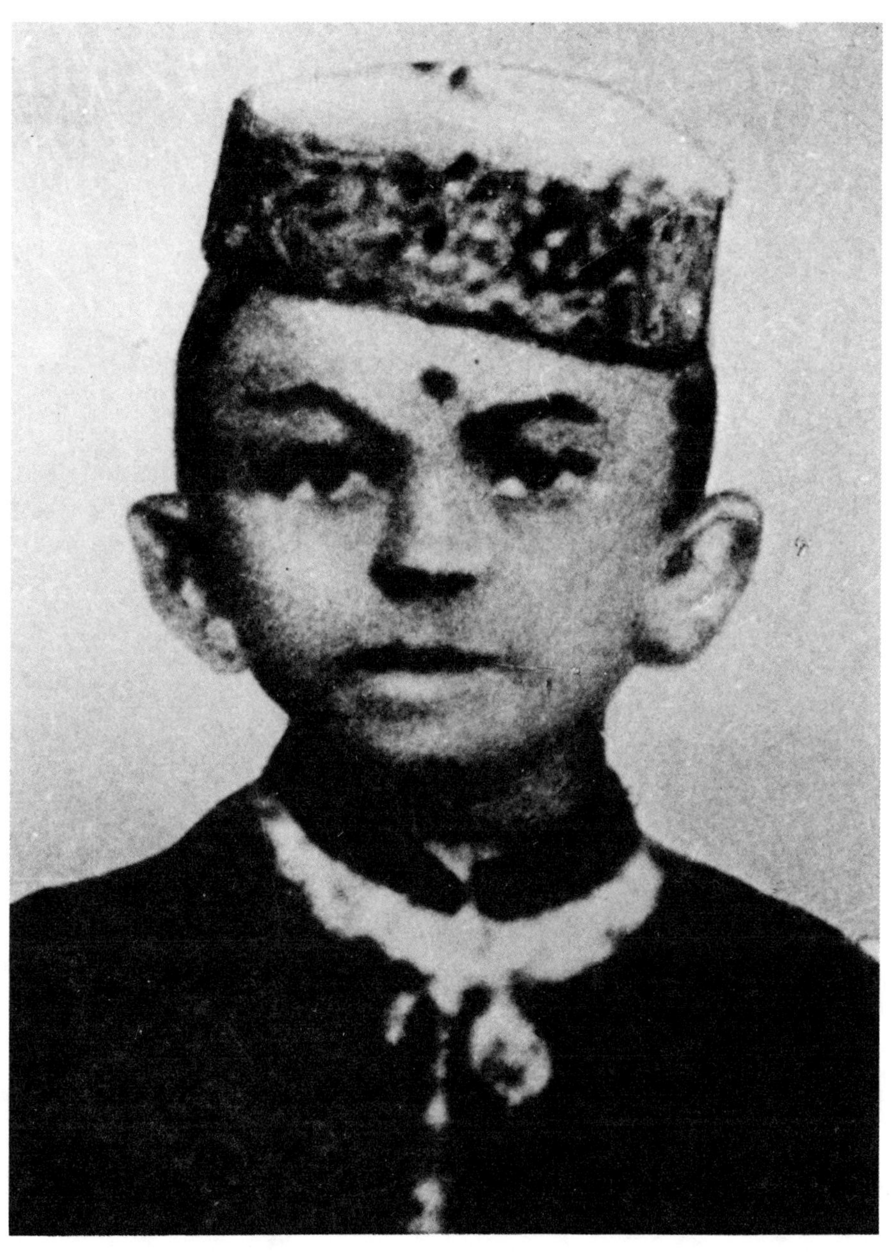

Gandhi at age seven

GANDHI
the Eternal Youth

George Ohsawa

Translated by Kenneth G. Burns

George Ohsawa Macrobiotic Foundation
Oroville, California

Originally published in Japanese in 1954. Translated into
French by Clim Yoshimi.

Photographs of Gandhi are used with the kind permission of
the National Gandhi Museum, New Delhi, India; quotations
from *An Autobiography or The Story of My Experiments with
Truth*, by M. K. Gandhi, the Navajivan Trust, Ahmedabad, India.

© Copyright 1986 by the
George Ohsawa Macrobiotic Foundation
1511 Robinson Street, Oroville, California 95965

Library of Congress Catalog Card Number: 86-080512
ISBN 0-918860-45-8

Contents

Publisher's Preface

In the early fifties a book written by working boys and girls called *Come Wind, Come Rain* was published. The lives and opinions of these young people attracted the attention of a number of educators. Among these educators was George Ohsawa, who had grown up as a working student.

Ohsawa loved working boys and girls so much that he wrote a book called *An Eternal Youth, Biography of Benjamin Franklin*, and donated all the royalties to them. This generous act on Ohsawa's part generated a reaction among the working youths, who created an organization of about two thousand members called Takenoko Kai (The Bamboo Shoot Association). Ohsawa responded by writing *Gandhi, the Eternal Youth* while on his way to India. He gave all the proceeds from this book to the working youth, as he had done with the publication of Franklin's biography.

Ohsawa wrote about Gandhi to encourage every young, poor worker to become a really great person like Gandhi. The conditions for becoming such a person were, for Ohsawa, to be healthy and not to lie. To be healthy, one must observe the macrobiotic diet, which can be explained as basically a vegetarian diet high in whole grains and low in fats and proteins. With this diet, however, one tries to balance the amounts of sodium and potassium both in food and in the blood. One who wants to know more about this diet should consult the many books written about it, some of which are included in the selected readings.

Foreword

As with most of my encounters with the works of Ohsawa, this one has an off-beat history. Talking to a friend recently, he informed me, "Oh yes, I have an unpublished work by Ohsawa. Are you interested in seeing it?"

"Yes," was my automatic response.

"Good, I'll have it here at the store; you can drop by and pick it up tomorrow."

That agreed on, I put this book at the back of my mind forgetting to go and pick it up the next day. The following day, two days after that conversation, I was rounding the bend in the stairs to my office/study, and there sitting in an alcove was *Gandhi: The Eternal Youth*, George Ohsawa, 1953.

There is more here than meets the eye. When I do not go to it, this book comes to me. I am a little, shall we say, superstitious, and, being so, I place a certain amount of stock in such occurrences.

For, in the beginning, I wasn't particularly anxious to immerse myself in any new Ohsawa writing. Partly because of the feeling, "I've heard all this before"; partly because after reading Ohsawa I always feel as though I've been through some kind of mind-scrambling device; and partly because I was afraid he was going to tell me something I didn't want to hear.

Gandhi did not disappoint me on any of these scores. This is "vintage" Ohsawa, saying what he always says, except this time (perhaps with the aid of the translation into French by Clim Yoshimi) more smoothly and cohesively. There is the usual element of mind-scrambling which occurs partly because the Japanese language in which Ohsawa thinks does not firmly fix such elements as tense, subject, and possessives; and partly because Ohsawa, although he schooled himself in Western logic, is not a logical thinker. He emphatically does not consider it to be the highest, most refined form of thought. The overall result is that subjects, moods and tenses have a discomforting tendency to slide into other subjects, moods and tenses – in the middle of a chapter, a page, a paragraph, in the middle of a sentence. Everything leaks into everything else. Even the category "biography" does not daunt Ohsawa in the least. This is not really a biography, or if it is one, it is almost as much a biography of Ohsawa as of Gandhi.

So far so good? (A favorite Ohsawian phrase.) But none of the foregoing is why I am translating this into English. Rather, the real subject matter of the book is *lying* and the many forms that it takes and the chaos it brings into our lives. Thus, much of what follows will seem old-fashioned – like something out of a Sunday school class. To some the thought revealed here may be so far removed that it seems inappropriate, or ridiculous, or even outrageous. "Hey, when is this guy going to stop? Can people, can anyone really ever have thought or felt like this?"

The reason why I am translating this work, then, is because in it Ohsawa tells me something I didn't want to hear but that I needed to hear: Everything is *not* relative. Everything does *not* change. Truth is *not* relative to the situation. This came as somewhat of a shock to me, for as an advanced student of "situational ethics" I had long thought that the correct behavior in any given situation or relationship was the one that created the most *harmony*. I prided myself on my skill in making balance in each new situation. And, if I had to say one thing one time and the exact opposite the next, that didn't bother me, for

this was not a question of "right" or "wrong," "true" or "false."
It did not occur to me that this approach might qualify as
doubletalk or doublethink; I had heard all about *1984*, and I was
on my guard against that. None of this "freedom is slavery,"
"love is hatred" stuff for me. But in my own way that's what I
was doing – until I encountered Ohsawa on Gandhi. With this
help I have been able to put aside my very finely calibrated
fence-straddling apparatus and go on to a new phase of life.

There is another reason for this translation, closely related
to the first: To a considerable extent, I had fashioned the approach to life described just above out of a misinterpretation of
Ohsawa's own principles. These principles were new to me, to
my culture, to my country, and I didn't know quite where to put
them, where they began, or where they ended. Therefore I
misused them just as I misused a car when I first learned to
drive.

But there was another cause for this misinterpretation. In
those first writings to be brought to these shores, Ohsawa concentrated on how to deal with this finite world of flux. And that
was good. *I owe my life to his well-timed advice.* But he did not
concretely spell out the relationship of this world where "everything changes" to that world where *nothing ever changes*, the
next world so to speak. And when that order is not clearly
spelled out, when that hierarchy is not firmly established, power
over the relative world can easily turn into manipulation or
even ruthless exploitation of it. For a time at least.

My second reason then for wanting to see this book in print
in English is that I think that it redresses the imbalance, that it
rounds out the picture. It adds a completely new and luminous
dimension to the teachings of George Ohsawa. I firmly believe
that it will help him take his rightful place as a world-class
thinker and philosopher.

I invite all and sundry to join in on this pilgrimage. By now most of us have tried everything else, so why not give this a chance? I believe what follows to be the missing link in the healing of this generation. *Warning:* But be prepared for some uncomfortable twists and turns in the road ahead.

I dedicate this translation to Andrea and Matthew Burns. I fervently hope that it may have one-half the impact on their lives that it has had on mine.

Kenneth G. Burns
Brookline, Massachusetts
10 December 1983

Preface

In this book you will learn about the childhood and adolescence of the great sage Gandhi.

Not only was Gandhi a timid, cowardly boy, but he was also slow-witted and clumsy at sports, which consequently he hated. Moreover, his handwriting was very poor; and he even committed theft.

If you were not a whimperer or a coward, were neither timid nor dull-witted, were good at sports, had good handwriting, and had never lied or stolen, then it would be a waste of your time to read this book. You will surely become greater than Gandhi.

On the other hand, if you are, as was Gandhi, a sad, weak, vulnerable youth, this book will be of much interest to you. For here you will discover how he was able to become such an outstandingly great person.

If you are even more miserable and pathetic than the young Gandhi, this book will be of still greater interest, for through reading it you will learn how to advance more easily along the Path than did he. This means that in this book you will encounter a practical method, a compass that points to God – another name for Truth. This Gandhi himself lost sight of many times, although he sought God all his life. And at the price of his life.

Since many meanings are given for this ancient word "Truth," I will define it: According to my understanding, Gandhi's Truth means the Order of the Universe, or the Unique Principle. To avoid all confusion, I frequently use the Unique Principle, or Practical Dialectics, or even the Magic Spectacles (for children) in place of the word Truth.

At last, within four or five days, I will set foot on the soil of the country that gave birth to Gandhi – India, the mother of the Far East. My heart is as full of joy as that of a schoolboy the night before the annual school trip.

George Ohsawa
Rangoon, Burma
4 November 1953

Gandhi as a lawyer in South Africa, age thirty-seven

Departure for India

The Mother of the Far East

"I have to write no matter what," I say to myself picking up my pen. Through the window, the blue-black sea and the grey sky alternately rise and fall. I am aboard the *Sadhana* sailing at a good speed toward the north of the Indian Ocean with Rangoon as the destination. My cabin, number 10, is a splendid, first-class accommodation. In several days I will arrive in Calcutta.

After thirty-nine years I am revisiting India, the country of Gandhi and the mother of the Far East. When I first went there in 1914, Gandhi was already completely immersed in the struggle to realize his grandiose ideal: the liberation of India and the Hindus. I was just a child then, a ninny who hadn't even heard of Gandhi. Because I knew a bit of French, I had been appointed the purser of a small ship. Prior to this trip, sad and poor, I had been living alone for several months on a small unemployment compensation in Kobe. That was the first time I had been reduced to such a state; I only had enough money to last me one month. It was as though my life were covered with thick, dark clouds; there wasn't the faintest flicker of the smallest star to show me the right direction.

But the Order of the Universe never fails: "Yin produces Yang," "the higher the mountain, the deeper the valley," "joy follows sorrow." Thus it was with one stroke that I was suddenly swept into a joyous world full of light. One fine day as I was preparing a meal of brown rice, a messenger dressed in the splendid uniform of the French Consulate came to my shabby little room in search of me. I was taken by this messenger to my former teacher of French, Mr. Kurihara.

"You want to go to France, don't you?" was the first thing he said when he saw me.

"Far from it, Sir, at the moment I'm unemployed. . . ."

"Good, then it is okay with you."

Mr. Kurihara was a very good and very affectionate teacher. Someday such a person will enter into your life. After I had become a messenger for an import-export company in Kobe, with two yen and lodging as salary, I had studied the French language for two hours a week at the French school where Mr. Kurihara was my teacher. A real Edokko (man of old Tokyo) from a traditional Samurai family, he invited me to his humble residence several times. I will never forget that cold winter night when he offered me *sobagaki*, a very thick buckwheat cream. I profoundly regret not having the chance to see him again before his death so that I might repay him for his kindness.

Mr. Kurihara liked me so much that, choosing me over four other classmates, he gave me the opportunity to take a clear-cut direction in my life. In my lifetime I have met many, many people who have demonstrated this kind of concern for me, but we were always separated after a short time together. When I search for a way to show gratitude towards them, a heavy feeling of oppression comes over me, and I feel as though I cannot breathe. It is this feeling that has impelled me to help with all my power those young people who at the threshold of life are riddled with sadness, loneliness, and suffering. In reality, it is thanks to the many people like Mr. Kurihara that I am writing this book and making this marvelous ocean voyage.

"You want to go to France, don't you? Well, here is your chance. And you can become ship purser if you want; all you have to do is go to the shipping company with this letter."

As if in a dream, I went to the maritime shipping company where I met Mr. Junpei Shirasu. "You understand French, and English too? And you know accounting? Very well, there is no problem." After this short, matter-of-fact interview, he promptly gave me a certificate of employment.

"The wages are not high, but you will receive a bonus when you return from the trip."

The salary was 80 yen, plus a wartime allowance – 240 yen! My joy at this unexpected, good news was so great that I lost my self-control. Hardly two months earlier I had been dismissed from my job with 25 yen unemployment compensation; and, with so little money in my pocket, I had fallen into a state of despair. And, a year before, I had been happy to receive a salary of 2 yen with lodging. *C'est la vie.* If I hadn't been fired from my job I would have missed this chance, for I was such a timid and cowardly young man that I wouldn't have dreamed of quitting it on my own.

That was thirty-nine years ago, that first trip to Europe, and it was as ship's purser that I crossed the sea. Since then I have crossed the ocean a score of times as a passenger, often third, fourth, or fifth class. This time I am a first-class passenger. That initial voyage lasted sixty days, the ship (a small packet boat of 1600 tons) picking up a load of rice at Saigon and transporting it to Marseilles. Today, this trip takes only thirty days.

Since departing the port of Kobe, dressed in simple Japanese costume, every day I have passed my time reading and writing.

As much as possible, I have been helping the helmsman in the scrubbing of the decks, and I have assisted with the cooking. In addition, I have played the role of doctor, and, in the case of a burial at sea, even that of a priest. (I was able to recite the *Shuniata* because I had been an apprentice in a Buddhist temple from the age of ten.)

From Japan to Singapore and even to Penang, the voyage was very calm. The smooth and tranquil sea was like an ebony mirror shining with silvery reflections. Especially at night it resembled an immense asphalt sports field. The moon and stars were visible. Then, since entering the Indian Ocean, there has been much wind and rain; and now the rolling of the ship has become rather violent. My wife, who had been so happy that the first trip of her life was going so smoothly, is now resting in bed, not going on deck since the ship entered stormy seas. When she does try to go on deck, she is unable to walk. Nearby, a Burmese woman vomits uncontrollably.

Many of the passengers are no longer going to the dining hall, while many of those who do are leaving it looking queasy after only a light meal. As for me, I feel no ill effects; and this is not because I have travelled by boat so much in the past thirty-nine years. As a matter of fact, from early youth on, because I was weak and sickly, I always suffered from seasickness on boats and trains. But, through the relentless practice of the Way of Life and the macrobiotic diet, I have finally become strong and healthy after forty years. It is especially those people who have weak stomachs that suffer from seasickness. Fortunately, I am no longer afflicted with this condition.

Above all, it is health that counts most in life; your life is spoiled if you don't feel well. Especially for someone like myself, who started the grand navigation of life without parents, money or education, health is the only capital and the only defense. Money, physical strength, and knowledge are all to no avail without health; and the best means of acquiring health is through correct daily eating. This is the macrobiotic diet that I have explained and taught for more than forty years. The method I call "macrobiotics" bears no resemblance to conventional health methods. It is the Way of Happiness and Freedom that humanity has been ardently but unsuccessfully trying to materialize for 300,000 years.

Even though a person has had great success in life, he will fall sick if he doesn't make a painstaking effort to discover, understand, and practice the Way of Happiness and Freedom. He will lose his teeth (those who have dental cavities are already defeated by the fifth round of the match); he will become nearsighted; or he will lose his wife and children. He will never come to understand that his success was useless in his life. In truth, in order to become a free and happy man, it is absolutely unnecessary to have money, great physical strength, fame, or knowledge. On the contrary, all this does nothing more than greatly contribute to the making of an unhappy slave.

Nevertheless, everyone, without exception, believes that the most important things in life are money, fame, learning, power, weapons, authority, good luck, security, etc. Because everyone else has those things, after all, it is quite natural to think that way. Thus, the have-nots of the world put their very lives on the line in the struggle to obtain them; otherwise, they consider their lives to be miserable. Even though these overly material values serve only to create a life of uncertainty, unhappiness, and slavery, nevertheless everyone – parents, teachers, and society – teach you the opposite: that they are indispensable conditions for achieving happiness. Moreover, a devil by the name of Greed, who loves the material things of life, is hiding himself at the bottom of your soul.

But all these conditions are necessary in order for you to attain true happiness and freedom. Thus, you will defeat that devil within you; you will leap over all these obstacles; and in the end you will achieve Absolute Justice, Eternal Happiness, and Infinite Freedom. Such a grand and amusing obstacle course is life. Therefore, in order to experience the supreme joy of finishing first in this fabulous race, you should not cling to money, fame, knowledge, weapons, security, and so forth. They are all nothing but traps.

God is equitable and just. God *is* justice. He places all of us at the starting line equally: without money, without fame, without power or weapons, without knowledge – without anything. A newborn baby has none of that. *But*, God is also mischievous. He sets out a trap in the form of a mountain of silver and gold before we have run a hundred yards. In the next two or three hundred yards, there is a mountain of knowledge; and a hundred yards later comes power and influence. After that there are mountains, forests, and rivers of pleasures: gastronomic delights, drinks, amusements, games, idle diversions, luxuries – "the good life" – pleasures of every description, every hundred yards. Then, right at the very end, he puts the biggest stumbling block of all: Glory. Even those who with great effort have lasted this far are stopped by this obstacle. Only one person in a million courageously leaps over it. But the victory in this race goes not only to him who leaps over this final hurdle, but also to those who follow him, who do not forget his words. Upon seeing his example, they will all attain it too.

Even he who runs last.

II

Gandhi's Secret

How Was He Created?

Gandhi is one of those who crossed the finish line in the obstacle course of life. For this attainment, health is indispensable. And this Gandhi had. In my work on Benjamin Franklin I outlined a method of achieving health that anyone, regardless of circumstances, can do without taking too much time or going to too great an expense. Since then, one year and two months have passed. During this time, by how much have you improved your health? Many have written me joyful letters announcing the cure of tuberculosis and nearsightedness; or they tell me that they no longer catch colds. But how are those people who have not written me doing?

At one time I was a bundle of sicknesses and shortcomings. I was a coward and a cry-baby; timid and extremely thin, I had a sickly complexion. In addition, I suffered from tuberculosis, hemorrhoids, nearsightedness, astigmatism, trachoma, prolapsed stomach, inflammation of the stomach, gastric dilatation, intestinal tuberculosis, scabies, many forms of eczema, etc. In fact, it would have been better for me to have started all over from the beginning. However, macrobiotics completely transformed the defective and vulnerable young boy that I was, and has allowed him to live up until today – to sixty years of age.

7

This is the philosophy of health that has caused me to distribute two million books, and to publish several magazines for thirty years. It has allowed me to help one hundred thousand sick people find a better way of life; it has enabled me to travel for over ten years in Japan and thirty abroad, where I have made ten voyages. Last but not least, it has allowed me to extend my life for forty years – forty years of amusing and joyful experiences that live in my memory.

However, at the age of sixty, my obstacle course is still not over. Lately I have not been satisfied with the difficulties I encounter in Japan. They are not big enough. Thus, in order to begin a new chapter in my life, I have left Japan with my wife on a voyage that will last until the day I die – with no home to return to. This never-ending odyssey will take me to the burning plateau of India, to Nepal in the frozen Himalayas, to the deserts of Africa, to snow-covered Sweden and Norway. As I begin this voyage there is great joy in my heart.

Already I am three or four thousand miles away from you, my dear students. The method of constructing the "flying carpet" that has brought me so far, the secret that has brought me such great happiness is macrobiotics. I presented you with this health method in the book, *An Eternal Youth – Biography of Benjamin Franklin*. What gave me the inspiration to write that little book, was your collection of writings, *Come Wind, Come Rain*.

In the first volume of *An Eternal Youth*, I wrote the biography of Benjamin Franklin – a Westerner. Now, in this second volume, I have chosen Gandhi, a Far-Easterner, for my subject. Although I have never met Gandhi, I will soon be in contact with Mr. Nehru and Mr. Bhave, who have been his disciples for more than thirty years. At a recent gathering in Tokyo to commemorate Gandhi's birthday, I met another disciple, Madame Swami Nataan. Like Nehru and Behave, this frail, weak woman, about fifty years old, spent a long period of time in prison with Gandhi. In the liberation of 357,000,000 Indians, and in the overthrow of the ferocious English regime that had lasted 150 years, these men and women accomplished something unparalleled in world history. And they did it, in large part, through the methods of total vegetarianism and total fasting – methods that are much more severe than my macrobiotic method.

Although Franklin was a great man, his effect on history is not on the same scale as Gandhi's. Therefore, this biography, which focuses on Gandhi's youth, will surely be much more difficult to relate than that of Franklin's. Since Romain Rolland wrote the first biography of Gandhi, dozens more have been written; but none of them reveals the inner mechanism that produced this great historic personality. That is the secret that would be most interesting to those who want to become as great as him; and that is what I am going to reveal. This, then, will be a physiological and biological history of which even the subject himself was not fully aware. The text I will use for reference is *An Autobiography, or The Story of My Experiments with Truth*, written by Gandhi himself.

In the future I would like to write the life histories of Vivekananda and Ramakrishna, the two great Indian philosophers. These two personalities, like Buddha, Nagarjuna or Renjun, are the predecessors of Gandhi. From the depths of the forests of India they perfected the ascetic way of absolute vegetarianism and pointed out the shortest path to Peace and Freedom. After that, I would like to tell the stories of such diverse personalities as George Bernard Shaw, Leo Tolstoy, Abraham Lincoln, and others who led a free and happy life while creating their own health through the practice of vegetarianism.

Now, since India is coming closer and closer, I must write this book as rapidly as possible. For, once I reach India, there won't be much time for writing. Day and night I will have great adventures to live through: the visa, the lack of adequate finances, employment, the English language, the heat. . . . And, in order to heal many sick people, I will have to teach the quickest way to Freedom and Happiness – that secret, subterranean passage that no one has found for 300,000 years. Ah, how many kinds of great difficulties await me!

After thinking it over, I have decided to write at least this one book. The rolling of the ship is so violent! The first hurdle of my obstacle course is already here.

III

He Who Can Convince Others

A Pure Sweet Mother, An Elegant Son

Gandhi's grandfather, a man of principles, was the Prime Minister of Kathiyavar, the big peninsula on the west side of India to the north of Bombay. He had six sons, the fifth of whom was Gandhi's father. For some time, Gandhi's father was also the Prime Minister. He married four times, death taking his wife each time. From his first and second marriages there resulted two daughters; his fourth wife gave him one daughter as well as three sons. The last son was our Gandhi.

> My father was a lover of his clan, truthful, brave, and generous, but short-tempered. To a certain extent he might have been given to carnal pleasures. For he married for the fourth time when he was over forty. But he was incorruptible and had earned a name for strict impartiality in his family as well as outside. . . .
>
> My father never had any ambition to accumulate riches and left us very little property.
>
> He had no education, save that of experience. . . . Of history and geography he was innocent. But his rich experience of practical affairs stood him in good stead in the solution of the most intricate questions and in managing hundreds of men. (M. K. Gandhi,

> *An Autobiography, or The Story of My Experiments
> with Truth*, 2nd ed., 1940, part I, chapter I. All fur-
> ther quotations cited are from *An Autobiography*; see
> Selected Readings for available editions.)

This is something that only an extremely capable man can do. There are many people who pass through an entire lifetime without being able to convince or to guide even one single person, in spite of being licensed or bearing the title of professor. Through the force of money or authority you cannot become a person who can convince others. It must be done through love – a love that causes other people to want to help you in return. How many persons have you been able to convince in your lifetime? In order to convince others, above all, you should have a wide field of action. How many friends can you count on at present? What is a friend? That's someone who is going in the same direction as you, who thinks as you do, and with whom you can always share the joys and sorrows of life. Unless you have friends of that kind, you cannot hope to convince one single person. And, in that case, you will never become truly happy.

In his last days Gandhi's father began reading the *Gita*, repeating aloud some verses every day at the time of worship. Even though religious readings may be incomprehensible to infants, what a beneficial influence Gandhi must have received from the well-ordered life of his father. These regular, daily recitations would have been useless if his father's conduct hadn't been in accordance with them.

What kind of woman was Gandhi's mother?

> The outstanding impression my mother has left on
> my memory is that of saintliness. She was deeply
> religious. She would not think of taking her meals

without her daily prayers. Going to *Haveli* – the Vaishnava temple – was one of her daily duties. As far as my memory can go back, I do not remember her having ever missed the *Chaturmas*. She would take the hardest vows and keep them without flinching. Illness was no excuse for relaxing them. (pt. I, ch. I)

Ah! A devout mother with a will of iron. An iron will is not dependent on formal education, position, money, faith, or religion. But, this strength of will, this orderly attitude in daily life, this serious truthfulness, this God-like exactitude, was the most important force in establishing the greatness of Gandhi.

During the last forty years I have lived with more than a thousand young people – some for several months, some for several years – treating them as though they were my own children. Out of all of them I know of only three who had the strength of will and pure elegance of Gandhi. In all the rest of them there was something prematurely old and churlish, something untidy, careless and sloppy. They were not orderly, nor were they in the habit of being exact. Even when they were well groomed, had taken good care of their hair and were well dressed, there was always something unclean in their faces. That was the impression you received at first glance.

And, if you worked with them for a day, you would understand even better: They allowed bits of food to fall on the floor while eating, chewed with their mouths open, and did not know how to use utensils correctly. But, above all, they were very clumsy when it came to cleaning. They did not know how to put their books in order on shelves, and the inside of their drawers looked as though someone had turned a garbage can over inside them. They transformed their writing table into a catch-all. The worst thing was their washing. Their underwear was dirtier after the washing than before it; and each time the fabrics shrank. Moreover, they were sloppy at ironing.

As for me, I am very skillful at washing and cooking, because from infancy on I was trained in those things both as a Buddhist temple boy and as an employee at a tobacco shop. In cleaning I yield to no one.

After the age of twenty I dressed in a garment with a high collar that at the time cost twelve yen. I brushed my clothes every day. And, in order to keep the pleat in my trousers, starting at the age of fourteen, I put them under my mattress every night. That's why my clothes have lasted me so many years without wearing out. One certain garment lasted me for over thirty years.

One day last year I showed a picture of myself, taken at the age of twenty-seven, to each of my students, asking them if there were anything identical to my dress of that day. Many students said, "The tie is the same." And that was correct. That tie had been given me by my first wife more than thirty years before when I was twenty-six. I lavish a great deal of care on things and objects; I love them with all my heart. I care for them, brushing, washing, and polishing them, so they will not wear out or be destroyed. I even repaint and redye them.

Let me give you an example of how much use I get out of an object: The fountain pen I am using for this book I bought in Tokyo for six yen thirty-five years ago when I was a bachelor. Six yen was a lot for me at that time because I was only making twelve yen a month. In the beginning this Waterman was covered with numerous, very fine inscriptions, but now they are completely worn away, leaving no trace. The pen is completely smooth. . . .

I have extolled myself at great length in order to introduce you to the idea of creativity. Every day we should create something new.

We should have the attitude that everything we touch with our hands, everything we see be transformed into beautiful, useful objects that bring joy to others. It is this unshakeable spirit, a spirit originating in the soul of the true mother, that creates all great men, all great sages. It inspires all of us to conceive of Infinite Freedom, Absolute Justice, and Eternal Peace. I believe that such a soul is the most important element in the world. It is the creative force in life.

Gandhi's mother is one person who had this creative attitude towards life. Another was my mother, who was twenty when I was born, and who died alone at the age of thirty. During those ten years she forged this creative force into my soul so deeply that after she died I was able to live through the most turbulent ten years of my life. My mother never attended school. And neither did the mother and father of Gandhi.

Now how about your situation?

You didn't have the conventional, prerequisite conditions? You didn't have parents, money, or protectors but, on the contrary, you had little brothers and sisters to care for? What an opportunity, what a joy! It is a marvel without equal. Even if you did not have parents like those of Gandhi, Franklin, or Lincoln, without them you can still straighten out your life. My mother, as well as Gandhi's mother, had so much work to do for their families that they didn't have time to teach the details to their children. They simply lived an orderly life which the children imitated and to which they became accustomed. Children who are still too young to have their own orientation in life will follow the orderly example of their parents.

Unhappy are those who have parents, especially the mother, who are negligent, who do not have order in their lives.

IV

The Mother Who Never Lies

The Liar Can Become a Non-Liar

To keep two or three consecutive fasts was nothing to her. Living on one meal a day during *Chaturmas* [a four-month period of fasting similar to a long lent] was a habit with her. Not content with that, she fasted every alternate day during one *Chaturmas*. During another *Chaturmas* she vowed not to have food without seeing the sun. We children on those days would stand, staring at the sky, waiting to announce the appearance of the sun to our mother. Everyone knows that at the height of the rainy season the sun often does not condescend to show his face. And I remember days when, at his sudden appearance, we would rush and announce it to her. She would run out to see with her own eyes, but by that time the fugitive sun would be gone, thus depriving her of her meal. "That does not matter," she would say cheerfully, "God did not want me to eat today." And then she would return to her round of duties. (pt. I, ch. I)

What an astounding and admirable education! This is real education. Parents and teachers may tell the children that they shouldn't lie every day for ten years; but that doesn't cause the children to tell the truth. Why? Because the teachers and parents are lying.

The majority of the young people I have known lie to one degree or another. Those who lie are ignorant of the truth and trample it underfoot; consequently, they cannot understand the world of Truth and Love. They are not qualified to amuse themselves in the world of Freedom, for, in reality, the world of Freedom is the world of Truth.

A sad habit is lying!

And it is from their parents that children learn this sad habit. Gandhi's mother was that rare person who did not lie – to herself, to God, to the children, or even to the dog. Children who have lived five or six years with such a mother never acquire the habit of lying even if they are educated by dishonest teachers. The parents, above all the mother, are the most decisive influence.

In the creation of a joyous world in which people do not lie, it is the mother, then, who plays the most important role. The children of a deceitful mother suffer a great deal; sometimes their lives are completely ruined. However, if these children can transform themselves into non-liars, they will experience an even greater joy than if their mother had raised them to be that way in the first place.

> My mother had strong common sense. She was well informed about all matters of State, and ladies of the court thought highly of her intelligence. Often I would accompany her, exercising the privilege of childhood, and I still remember many lively discussions she had with the widowed mother of the Thakore Saheb. (pt. I, ch. I)

In my opinion, education is complete before the age of five or six. After that age, education consists only of techniques and information. It is reasonable to say, then, that a person's happiness or unhappiness – whether he becomes a free man or a fallen outcast – depends almost totally on the mother. The mother who lies is negligent and disorderly in daily life. Once she has told one lie, another must be invented to cover up the first; and the lies grow proportionately bigger. Sooner or later this must end in unhappiness.

To be sure, he who tells a lie, but who can transform what he has said into the truth, is not truly a liar. On the contrary, it is he whose actions are not in accordance with his words who is a liar. That is why there are some great liars who have technically never lied in their lives. In contrast with them, I have a much higher esteem for those persons who, throughout their entire lives, make every effort to materialize what they have said, even if it was, technically, a lie.

Let me try to illustrate this situation. There are two kinds of non-drinkers: those who dislike and cannot drink alcohol from birth; and those who, previously drunks, have overcome alcohol after many defeats. Those who are temperate since birth, who do not know alcohol, do not know how to cure alcoholism. In contrast, those who went right to the bottom with alcohol, and came close to ruining their lives with it, know how to help other alcoholics.

It is the same with lying. Let's suppose that, unfortunately, you are a liar. How happy people will be if you transform yourself into a non-liar! I know a method of curing the sickness of lying. I, too, used to be a liar. Some people say that I still am. Since I was young I have announced various dreams that I have not been able to materialize: "I will go to France," "I will become a writer," etc. And even today I often tell falsehoods such as "I will create a world government," or "I will take a trip around the world," etc. Because all these projects seem impossible, people take me for a liar.

I am not a great and eminent man as was Gandhi. As I have said, I was a boy with a weak will and a sickly body, and I am still a pitiful child. But, all my life I have made every effort to make my falsehoods come true. And it is thanks to my method of macrobiotics that I have been able to pursue these efforts.

V

The Young Gandhi

Whimperer, Coward, Dullard

I was born at Porbandar, otherwise known as Suda-mapuri, on the 2nd of October, 1869. (pt. I, ch. I)

Take note of this date, 2nd of October, and try to read the books written about Gandhi on it. It is an excellent practice to read about the lives of great persons in the same month as they were born.

> It was with some difficulty that I got through the multiplication tables. The fact that I recollect nothing more of those days than having learnt, in company with other boys, to call our teacher all kinds of names, would strongly suggest that my intellect must have been sluggish, and my memory raw. (pt. I, ch. I)

Could it be that Gandhi is a person who never lies? How this history of honest recollections encourages us! This simple act of not lying, of relating a fact as it really happened, gives great joy and strength to numerous people.

> I must have been about seven when my father left Porbandar for Rajkot to become a member of the Rajasthanik Court. There I was put into a primary school, and I can well recollect those days, including

21

> other particulars of the teachers who taught me. As at
> Porbandar, so here, there is hardly anything to note
> about my studies. I could only have been a mediocre
> student. From this school I went to the suburban
> school and thence to the high school, having already
> reached my twelfth year. I do not remember having
> ever told a lie, during this short period, either to my
> teachers or my schoolmates. (pt. I, ch. II)

So! Young Gandhi was a boy who did not lie. As for myself, I don't dare declare that so definitely. Although my mother was a person who never lied, my father was a liar. That's the reason I cannot say that I didn't lie. My father abandoned my mother after five years of marriage. How this young mother must have suffered living all alone with her children, forced to do manual labor every day. I cannot forget the deplorable expression on her face during that period. Whatever the reason for it may be, abandoning or divorcing a mate is a great falsehood; for each party swears at the beginning of the marriage that they will make every effort to give the spouse a happy life.

> I used to be very shy and avoided all company. My
> books and my lessons were my sole companions. To
> be at school at the stroke of the hour and to run back
> home as soon as the school closed – that was my daily
> habit. I literally ran back, because I could not bear to
> talk to anybody. I was even afraid lest anyone should
> poke fun at me. (pt. I, ch. II)

Young Gandhi was such a timid boy. On that point, I was no different. I was probably even more timid than Gandhi.

> There is an incident which occurred at the examina-
> tion during my first year at the high school and which
> is worth recording. Mr. Giles, the Educational Inspector,

had come on a visit of inspection. He had set us five words to write as a spelling exercise. One of the words was "kettle." I had mis-spelt it. The teacher tried to prompt me with the point of his boot, but I would not be prompted. It was beyond me to see that he wanted me to copy the spelling from my neighbor's slate, for I had thought that the teacher was there to supervise us against copying. The result was that all the boys, except myself, were found to have spelt every word correctly. Only I had been stupid. The teacher tried later to bring this stupidity home to me, but without effect. I never could learn the art of "copying."

Yet the incident did not in the least diminish my respect for my teacher. I was by nature blind to the faults of elders. Later I came to know of many other failings of this teacher, but my regard for him remained the same. For I had learnt to carry out the orders of elders, not to scan their actions. (pt. I, ch. II)

This is an extremely important point. It is highly disadvantageous to accuse, let alone slander, despise, protest, or to attack the shortcomings of elders, seniors, and others in general. On this point, too, I will cede nothing to Gandhi, for my mother taught me to respect not only every kind of person but even dogs and birds. As a child I was brought up to see only the good side of people. I cannot recall my mother ever saying anything bad about another person. She never even slandered or complained about my father who abandoned her. This was not an attitude that she unwillingly forced upon herself; on the contrary, her feeling was that the shortcoming lay with her, that it was her fault that her husband had not been satisfied. In general, she blamed herself and suffered the consequences when others became liars or traitors.

To many this attitude may seem of little importance, but in

reality, it is crucially important. The mentality that finds the cause of all unhappiness in one's self is the mentality that, transcending all antagonistic relationships, sees the entire world and itself as one. This is possible only for those who have a total understanding of the Order of the Universe. I received this mentality from my mother; Gandhi received it from his father as well as from his mother.

This thinking represents the high-point of all religions. Every man who has devoted his life to bringing peace and freedom to humanity – every great man – possesses this mentality from infancy.

He who demonstrates slander, hate, and scorn towards others is showing that he has an arrogant, exclusive, and egotistical character. Such a person will never be able to learn anything from others and will end up hated and unhappy. The mother who easily and freely expresses slander, scorn, and feelings of hate, unknowingly drags her children into the stream of an unhappy life. In her ignorance, she is causing them to be defeated by life. To give them a formal education later on, no matter how costly, is futile.

A mother who curses, slanders, or expresses feelings of scorn – even once – is the cause of unhappiness.

If you had such a mother, you must be leading a sad life, for she sold you to the devil. This is an unparalleled misfortune. In this case you should escape from the bad habit you inherited from her at all costs. It is, however, extremely difficult. Try, and if you succeed, teach me your method.

VI

Negligence Becomes a Falsehood

The Liar Is Created by a Wrong Education

During this youthful period of his life, Gandhi's imagination was excited by a book, and by a traveling theatrical group.

> Somehow my eyes fell on a book purchased by my father. It was *Shravana Pitribhakti Nataka* (a play about Shravana's devotion to his parents). I read it with intense interest. There came to our place about the same time itinerant showmen. One of the pictures I was shown was of Shravana carrying, by means of slings fitted for his shoulders, his blind parents on a pilgrimage. The book and the picture left an indelible impression on my mind. "Here is an example for you to copy," I said to myself. (pt. I, ch. II)

This painful story made such an impression on him that he remembered it right to the end of his life.

At about the same period in his life, he saw another spectacle, "Harishchandra"; and he began to ask himself the following grandiose question: "Why should not all be truthful like Harishchandra?" (pt. I, ch. II) As a boy, Gandhi often cried when he read books or saw plays.

The shadow of sadness and suffering was already stealthily approaching Gandhi's happy adolescence. In that part of India it was the custom for the parents to arrange an engagement when the child was seven, and to have him marry at about the age of thirteen. Accordingly, at the age of thirteen Gandhi was married, much to his regret to the end of his days. All his life, Gandhi blamed his premature marriage on himself, even though it had been imposed on him by his parents.

> I was devoted to my parents. But no less was I devoted to the passions that flesh is heir to. I had yet to learn that all happiness and pleasure should be sacrificed in devoted service to my parents. . . . Nishkulanand sings: "Renunciation of objects, without the renunciation of desires, is short-lived, however hard you may try." (pt. I, ch. III)

To have such a thought at the age of thirteen! What a prodigious people! As for me, not only at the age of twenty, but even now at the age of sixty, I find it very difficult to make such a rigorous self-criticism.

Have you read the novel *Gora* by Tagore? If not, look for it without delay in the bookstores or libraries. Through this novel you will find out how profound is the philosophy of the young people of India. Even though you will feel embarrassed by the comparison, you will learn a lot.

> I never took part in any exercise, cricket or football, before they were made compulsory. . . . I may mention, however, that I was none the worse for abstaining from exercise. That was because I had read in books about the benefits of long walks in the open air, and having liked the advice, I had formed a habit of taking walks, which has still remained with me. (pt. I, ch. V)

I also did not like sports. Of course, it is true that I also did not have the time or money for them, and when I did have a bit of each, it was reading that attracted me more.

> Now it so happened that one Saturday, when we had school in the morning, I had to go from home to the school for gymnastics at 4 o'clock in the afternoon. I had no watch, and the clouds deceived me. Before I reached the school the boys had all left. The next day Mr. Gimi, examining the roll, found me marked absent. Being asked the reason for absence, I told him what had happened. He refused to believe me and ordered me to pay a fine of one or two annas.
>
> I was convicted of lying! That deeply pained me. How was I to prove my innocence? There was no way. I cried in deep anguish. I saw that a man of truth must also be a man of care. This was the first and last instance of my carelessness in school. (pt. I, ch. V)

Again, what an extraordinary power of self-criticism. He had been scolded and punished by mistake, and he profited even from this by discovering a method to transform himself. He didn't blame the director, and he felt no inner hatred towards him. It is a very progressive mentality that can find the material for self-improvement even in the mistakes of others.

My principle in life is exactly the same. My rule is, "no excuses, no pardons." I do not ask for pardons, I make no excuses. I accept, without hesitation, any punishment or any condemnation. Even when, by mistake, I am insulted, punished, or disfigured, I always judge it to be my actions that were the cause.

In the past forty years I have been summoned by the police, by public prosecutors, and by military tribunals dozens of times; and I can no longer count the number of times I have been in prison. During the war, in December 1944, I was cruelly tortured and threatened with death because of my pacifist efforts. I was in prison from January to September, 1945, even after the war had been over for a month. After the war, falsely accused of "militarism," I was banned from public activity. During this time, in spite of many orders to do so, I did not submit a deposition to the prosecutor's office. Finally called before the highest judicial office, I offered no excuse – I didn't even say "Good day."

A man does only what he judges to be just. It does sometimes happen that his judgment is defective, but that is the fault of his education, not the fault of the person.

Often parents, schools, and even governments exercise low judgment. For instance, at present thousands of bags of rice are illegally transported to Tokyo every day by black-marketers. This is a living example of an unjust situation that has resulted from a defect in judgment on the part of the State. These dealers are doing that work because it is impossible for them to find a better way to make a living. Were it the case of a disaster caused by an earthquake or a famine, this activity would not be judged a crime. Instead, the State would be obligated to publicly praise those responsible for it. Actually, it is a violation of the constitution to restrict the freedom of a people by condemning such courageous activities. It is true that it was because of the war that it was necessary to institute such a law, but that same war was started by the government.

Such public errors, committed in broad daylight, are innumerable; therefore society is full of injustices that should be corrected. For that reason, courageous people, capable of convincing others, should attempt to reconstruct society. The opportunities to make yourself a free and great man are infinite.

VII

A Boy Clumsy at Writing

Better Neat Handwriting Than Pretty

. . . I do not know whence I got the notion that good
handwriting was not a necessary part of education,
but I retained it until I went to England. When later,
especially in South Africa, I saw the beautiful handwriting of lawyers and young men born and educated
in South Africa, I was ashamed of myself and repented
of my neglect. (pt. I, ch. V)

I, too, did not like to practice handwriting; and, even at present,
I am still very clumsy at it – to the point that I am disgusted
with myself. Also, I think that bad handwriting gives the reader
a disagreeable sensation. And I have discovered the reason for
that sensation: Poor handwriting stems from poor health. It is
proof that the writer's health is poor. Specifically, those who
have bad handwriting are not sociable. (This is my fifth condition of health.) Through practice, yin people develop a relatively good script more easily than do yang people. That is why
I have often allowed myself to be fooled by people who have
beautiful handwriting. Now I know that the person who tries to
write clearly, cleanly and legibly is more worthy of trust than
someone who has a pretty handwriting. Thus, by all means,
those people with sloppy, illegible handwriting should change

themselves as soon as possible.

> It is now my opinion that in all Indian curricula of
> higher education there should be a place for Hindi,
> Sanskrit, Persian, Arabic, and English, besides of
> course the vernacular. (pt. I, ch. V)

This is a difficult problem. In Japan we have learned that even after ten years of study, we are not able to handle English fluently. In contrast, the American soldiers learn fluent Japanese in six months. It takes only three years of studies for the officers to be able to read Japanese classics such as *Genji Monogatori*. And, as far as calligraphy is concerned, at the end of this time they write freely in block letters, running script, or semi-running script. However, in Japan a good method for learning foreign languages has still not been developed. Besides, the young people are still not courageous enough to learn them. This is because they are not in good health.

After having spent many long years in Europe studying foreign languages so that I could write books in them, I am convinced that no other field of study so clearly shows the condition of one's health as does the study of a language.

VIII

The Friend, Meat, and a Dream

The Day Dream and the Night Dream

While Gandhi was still a schoolboy, the modern, Western way of life began to unfold out into the provinces. Thus, he was surprised and hurt when he began hearing such rumors as: "Many of our teachers secretly eat meat and drink wine." "Many well-known people in the area are doing the same; and even students at school have taken part in it." A close friend explained these matters to him in this way:

> "We are a weak people because we do not eat meat. The English are able to rule over us, because they are meat-eaters. You know how hardy I am, and how great a runner too. It is because I am a meat-eater. Meat-eaters do not have boils or tumors, and even if they sometimes happen to have any, these heal quickly. Our teachers and other distinguished people who eat meat are no fools. They know its virtues. You should do likewise. There is nothing like trying. Try and see what strength it gives. . . . "
>
> This friend's exploits cast a spell over me. He could run long distances and extraordinarily fast. He was skillful at high and long jumping. He could put up with any amount of corporal punishment. He would

31

often display his exploits to me and, as one is always dazzled when he sees in others the qualities that he lacks himself, I was dazzled by this friend's exploits. This was followed by a strong desire to be like him. I could hardly jump or run. Why should not I be as strong as he? . . .

A doggerel of the Gujarati poet Narmad was in vogue amongst us schoolboys as follows:

> *Behold the mighty Englishman*
> *He rules the Indian small,*
> *Because being a meat-eater*
> *He is five cubits tall.*

All this had its due effect on me. I was beaten. It began to grow on me that meat-eating was good, that it would make me strong and daring, and that, if the whole country took to meat-eating, the English could be overcome.

A day was thereupon fixed for beginning the experiment. . . . The opposition to and abhorrence of meat-eating that existed in Gujarat among the Jains and Vaishnavas were to be seen nowhere else in India or outside in such strength. These were the traditions in which I was born and bred. And I was extremely devoted to my parents. I knew that the moment they came to know of my having eaten meat, they would be shocked to death. Moreover, my love of truth made me extra cautious. I cannot say that I did not know then that I should have to deceive my parents if I began eating meat. But my mind was bent on the "reform." . . . I wished to be strong and daring and wanted my countrymen also to be such, so that we might defeat the English and make India free. (pt. I, ch. VI)

So the day came. It is difficult fully to describe my

condition. There were, on the one hand, the zeal for "reform," and the novelty of making a momentous departure in life. There was, on the other, the shame of hiding like a thief to do this very thing. I cannot say which of the two swayed me more. We went in search of a lonely spot by the river, and there I saw, for the first time in my life – meat. There was baker's bread also. I relished neither. The goat's meat was as tough as leather. I simply could not eat it. I was sick and had to leave off eating.

I had a very bad night afterwards. A horrible nightmare haunted me. Every time I dropped off to sleep it would seem as though a live goat were bleating inside me, and I would jump up full of remorse. But then I would remind myself that meat-eating was a duty and so become more cheerful. . . .

I got over my dislike for bread, forswore my compassion for the goats, and became a relisher of meat-dishes, if not of meat itself. This went on for about a year. But not more than half a dozen meat feasts were enjoyed in all. . . .

Whenever I had occasion to indulge in these surreptitious feasts, dinner at home was out of the question. My mother would naturally ask me to come and take my food and want to know the reason why I did not wish to eat. . . .

Therefore I said to myself: "Though it is essential to eat meat, and also essential to take up food 'reform' in the country, yet deceiving and lying to one's father and mother is worse than not eating meat. In their lifetime, therefore, meat-eating must be out of the question. When they are no more and I have found my freedom, I will eat meat openly, but until that moment arrives I will abstain from it."

> This decision I communicated to my friend, and I
> have never since gone back to meat. (pt. I, ch. VII)

It was a child of twelve or thirteen that was defeated in this painful struggle. In his place would you have been able to act in the way he did? If not, you are not a person who is capable of accomplishing an undertaking as great as the one that Gandhi accomplished. However, if you wish to make such great efforts, conscientiously read this book several times. I am writing it for young men and women who want to accomplish great things.

Yielding to the temptation offered by his friend, Gandhi ignored the traditional taboo on eating meat. But, saying the fault was his, he never blamed it on that friend – thus freeing himself from the consequences of his transgression. He who does not discover that all weaknesses and sins are produced from within will never be able to overcome them. Consequently, when someone finds fault with you, you should not automatically respond with the pretext that he is mistaken. Even if the criticism is in error, it will not be to your advantage to protest or to give quick excuses. If, for any reason, someone accuses you, it is always your fault that he has done so.

After his terrible experiences with eating meat, Gandhi confessed the pain and suffering he felt at not being able to sleep peacefully. After forty years of study and experience, I have come to the conclusion that dreaming at night is a very unhealthy sign. It means that the nervous system is not sleeping and resting when it should be; and in this state of unnatural activity it produces false images or mirages.

Those people who cannot read books, who easily forget what they read, who are not attentive, who tire easily, who often fall ill, who are suspicious, who have few friends, who have no will, who are dull-witted, lead an unhappy, meaningless life devoid of freedom. All of them dream at night.

Dreaming during sleep is a mental derailment – a mild mental illness. Or rather, it is the first step towards a deep mental illness – one that may well result in an unhappy life. Again, once and for all, I will declare that dreaming is a sickness – a mental illness or a derangement of the nervous system. I can give a prescription for the cure of the sickness of dreaming. Just as I know how to cure insomnia and sleeping sickness, I know a method that will bring about a quiet and peaceful sleep without dreams – a sleep that erases fatigue and that creates a lively, fresh energy in the body. I will not explain this method here in detail because there is little time, but I will tell you where to find the key to this secret so that you can unlock it for yourselves.

This method involves a study of dreams. First of all, you should make a diary of your daily food and your dreams. In so doing you will come to know which kind of food produces which kind of dream. Be sure to include both the quality and the quantity of the food and drink that you take. In a few years you will be able to say in advance: "Ah, tonight I am going to have such and such a dream."

Sad, absurd, and frightening dreams are all caused by a poor diet, by an unhealthy way of feeding oneself. As long as you are dreaming at night you will not be able to work and study as you should during the day. You will not have good ideas, and, as a result, your life will not be brilliant. There, that is all I'm going to tell you about night dreams. With the clues I have given you here, you will be able to find out the rest on your own.

The dream you have in the daytime, when your consciousness is clear, is very good. This type of dream, what we might call a daydream, is thought directed towards such matters as how to achieve Absolute Justice, Eternal Happiness, and Infinite Freedom.

Also, it is very good to have another kind of dream, the one that is sometimes called a "true dream." This is one that concretely communicates to you an event that will happen in the future, or one that is happening at that moment in some far-away place: to dream of the sickness of your parents, the injury of your brother, visits from your friends, or a solution to a problem which has concerned you. This happens only when you are detached completely from desire and lust – when your mind is a vacuum. There is a very significant Chinese saying:

The Sages have no other dreams
Except for the dream that is real.

IX

How to Conquer Temptation

Have a Great Dream

A while later, accompanied by his friend, who had made the
arrangements and had paid the bill in advance, Gandhi went to
a house of ill-repute. However, he fled from this place without
having been unfaithful to his wife.

> From a strictly ethical point of view, all these occa-
> sions must be regarded as moral lapses; for the carnal
> desire was there, and it was as good as the act. But
> from the ordinary point of view, a man who is physi-
> cally saved from committing a sin is regarded as saved.
> And I was saved only in that sense. . . . As we know
> that a man often succumbs to temptation, however
> much he may resist it, we also know that Providence
> often intercedes and saves him in spite of himself.
> How all this happens, – how far a man is free and
> how far a creature of circumstances, – how far free-
> will comes into play and where fate enters on the
> scene, – all this is a mystery and will remain a mys-
> tery. (pt. I, ch. VII)

Now these are some really big questions. Gandhi was in his
fifties when he wrote this, and he confesses that at the time he
still did not know the nature of *will* and *freedom* as opposed to

37

circumstances and *fate.*

As for myself, making a great effort, I contemplated the order in which judgment develops and was able to discover seven stages. In so doing, I was able to unveil the mystery of human judgment. Recently, in several magazine articles, I wrote that the most essential role that my method of health plays is that of strengthening the will, judgment, ability to act, understanding, and memory – so that everyone may enter into the world of Freedom. I deeply regret that I will not be able to hear Gandhi's opinions and criticisms of these ideas. But, in his place, Mr. Nehru or Mr. Bhave may be able to help me.

At this stage in the writing, the boat has finally arrived at Rangoon. The appearance of this country is much different than it was thirty-nine years ago. According to the explanation given to me by an Englishman, the reason for this is that, although Burma has achieved independence, there is open conflict in the interior. India also split into two parts after achieving independence. In both cases this is the result of clouded, derailed judgment.

If you do not have the ambition to become as great as Gandhi, it is because you have neither a dream as big as his nor his sense of justice. In other words, you do not have high judgment. Your judgment is only at the second or third level.

Your level of judgment, whatever it may be, has already decided your life. Whether happy or unhappy, man's life decisively follows the ideals of childhood and adolescence. If your great ideal is a world of Freedom and Happiness, you will one day be able to enter into it. But, if that is not your goal, then I am broken-hearted. There is nothing that can be done.

Childhood dreams are very important; without fail, the grandiose dream will be realized. The dream of Jacques Mandes Daguerre was of this kind. By the light that glances from the window, the pretty scenery outside is reflected on a screen. Daguerre wanted to invent a system to capture this image on a piece of paper. Twenty years later, in the form of photography, this dream was realized. That's why the original name for photo in French was "Daguerrotype."

The dream of young Isaac Newton was to solve the mystery of the falling apple. This dream became the concept of universal gravitation that has reigned triumphant at the Academy of Physics for over two hundred years.

Heinrich Schliemann, archeologist and German Hellenist, dreamed of excavating the Greek cities of the Golden Age, and finding treasures. In discovering Troy, he realized his dream.

At the age of five, Kettering dreamed of finding out why leaves are green. He discovered the existence of chlorophyll, and seventy years later he became an eminent member of the American atomic research team.

Kenny, a young girl from the Australian countryside, dreamed of saving unfortunate children afflicted with polio. In order to devote herself to this dream, she abandoned her fiance and gave up all the pleasures of life. Although she did not find the cure for polio, she was named "woman of the century" and given a royal welcome in the United States.

Edner, a young mother, fought to have the term "bastard," which was making life difficult for millions of children, erased from American law. She succeeded. Her sad but beautiful story became the film, *Flower in the Dust*.

Florence Nightingale, the model for nurses . . .

Helen Keller, who surmounted the triple handicap of being blind, deaf, and mute . . .

Marie Curie, the poor student who discovered radium . . .

Paganini, the young itinerant musician . . .

Edison, who was thought to be an idiot, never finished school, and who sold newspapers to make a living, yet eventually became the greatest inventor in the world . . .

Lincoln, who, because of poverty could not buy books and was able to attend school for only six months, but who, becoming president of the United States, created the greatest democracy on earth . . .

Goodyear, who invented rubber . . .

These are but a few examples of people who had a great dream, a dream they conceived of while still children.

So! What luminous and joyful dream do you have?

If your dream is small and petty, it would be better to abandon it right now. Only on the condition that you have a big dream will I show you how to find Aladdin's magic lamp. With this lamp you will discover the secret of Ali Baba's magic – Open Sesame – and you will be able to make any dream come true.

X

The Hindu Woman and Wife

Self-Criticism Leads to Happiness

Although it was thanks to his mother that Gandhi became a great historical figure, the infinite patience and tolerance, the profound capacity for love of the Hindu woman and wife are still not widely known and appreciated.

Gandhi's wife was also a remarkable personality. Because he suspected her of being untrue, Gandhi treated her badly when he was young. This he regretted all the rest of his life. Knowingly or unknowingly a person casually commits a sin – a sin that can never be erased. The realization of this is extremely painful. But only those who never pardon themselves for their own transgressions and who, moreover, repent for them eternally can enter into the world of Freedom and Happiness. Those who say, "Excuse me," convinced that with these words their sins are forgiven, only to repeat the same actions the following day; those who don't bother even to excuse themselves; and those who, on the contrary, put the blame on their adversaries. All of them eternally repeat the same sins. Thus, without noticing it, every day they fall further into the depths of unhappiness.

Reform is impossible for those who do not practice deep and severe self-criticism. And, for those who cannot reform themselves, creativity is out of the question. Gandhi, to be sure, was a man of thoroughgoing self-criticism.

> One of the reasons of my differences with my wife was undoubtedly the company of this friend. I was both a devoted and a jealous husband, and this friend fanned the flame of my suspicions about my wife. I never could doubt his veracity. And I have never forgiven myself the violence of which I have been guilty in having pained my wife by acting on his information. Perhaps only a Hindu wife would tolerate these hardships, and that is why I have regarded woman as an incarnation of tolerance. A servant wrongly suspected may throw up his job, a son in the same case may leave his father's roof, and a friend may put an end to the friendship. The wife, if she suspects her husband, will keep quiet, but if the husband suspects her, she is ruined. Where is she to go? A Hindu wife may not seek divorce in a law-court. Law has no remedy for *her*. And I can never forget or forgive myself for having driven my wife to that desperation. . . . (pt. I, ch. VII)

XI

Gandhi Commits Theft

I, Too, Have Stolen

A relative and I became fond of smoking. Not that we saw any good in smoking, or were more enamored of the smell of a cigarette. We simply imagined a sort of pleasure in emitting clouds of smoke from our mouths. . . . But we had no money. So we began pilfering stumps of cigarettes thrown away by my uncle.

The stumps, however, were not always available, and could not emit much smoke either. So we began to steal coppers from the servant's pocket money in order to purchase Indian cigarettes. . . .

But we were far from satisfied with such things as these. Our want of independence began to smart. It was unbearable that we should be unable to do anything without the elders' permission. At last, in sheer disgust, we decided to commit suicide!

But how were we to do it? From where were we to get the poison? We heard that *Dhatura* seeds were an effective poison. Off we went to the jungle in search of these seeds, and got them. Evening was thought to be the auspicious hour. We went to *Kedarji Mandir*, put ghee in the temple-lamp, had the *darshan* and then looked for a lonely corner. But our courage failed us. Supposing we were not instantly killed? And what

43

was the good of killing ourselves? Why not rather put up with the lack of independence? But we swallowed two or three seeds nevertheless. We dared not take more. Both of us fought shy of death, and decided to go to *Ramji Mandir* to compose ourselves, and to dismiss the thought of suicide. . . .

The thought of suicide ultimately resulted in both of us bidding goodbye to the habit of smoking stumps of cigarettes and of stealing the servant's coppers for the purpose of smoking.

Ever since I have been grown up, I have never desired to smoke and have always regarded the habit of smoking as barbarous, dirty and harmful. I have never understood why there is such a rage for smoking throughout the world. I cannot bear to travel in a compartment full of people smoking. I become choked. (pt. I, ch. VIII)

So! The great Gandhi committed theft. And, forty-five years later, when he was known the world over as the messiah of 350,000,000 Hindus, he made it public. This is something that very few people are capable of doing.

Inspired by Gandhi's example, I will make a confession to you. After the death of my mother when I was ten, I became a temple-boy. Then, at the age of fourteen, my father, who had caused the death of my mother, reappeared with his mistress, whom I had to accept as a stepmother. My father, at the end of his resources, had to take in three or four students. My mother took care of them while my father did supplementary work. Every morning before the others were up, I cooked the rice; then I had to clean the house inside and out, clean five or six lamps, and then serve breakfast. Only after I had done all that could I go, half on the run, to school.

As soon as I was back home from school, I glued envelopes

to pay for school expenses, then put the kitchen in order. This was a difficult time for me because I had no room to study in. The students occupied three rooms leaving only the vestibule and the living room for the use of the family. And at night the family slept in the living room. That left the kitchen as the sole refuge during the day. In this situation I finally ended up studying in the bathroom by a small light after everyone else had gone to sleep.

Making envelopes hardly covered school expenses, so I couldn't afford books, even used books. So, I spent my summer and winter vacations copying the texts of history, geography, and English that I would need for the coming courses. Thus, my grade school studies were done almost completely on my own. This had the unexpected result of strengthening me. At any rate, after vacation, I hardly had time to study, except for two or three hours after the others had gone to sleep.

During that epoch of my life, I stole ten-sen coins five or six times from the rooms of the students when I cleaned them on Sundays and holidays. I hesitated a long time before I stole twenty-sen coins, but I did that a few times too. In those days a used book cost about five sen.

In addition, I often stole books from bookstores. Later, when I obtained a library card for the Kyoto library near my home, it became unnecessary for me to steal money or books. Still, even today, the memory of those thefts is painful to me. As a result of this, after the age of twenty I have never felt ill will towards anyone who has stolen from me. I even feel a touch of joy, especially when it is a book that has been stolen. I pardon the thefts of others, not out of generosity or love, but because *I* have committed theft.

For that same reason – because I have stolen – I like to give things to people. Those people who don't need anything, that I cannot give something to, embarrass me considerably. Through the act of giving thousands, tens of thousands of presents during the last forty years, I have tried to pay back what I stole when I was fifteen. Still, I don't think the sins of my childhood have been erased.

But there has been at least one result: I have discovered the secret of the art of giving pleasure to others through offering them gifts. Here are the essentials: 1. Give with the feeling that you are paying back for one ten-thousandth of the sins you have committed. 2. Give so that your present evokes a pleasure that has an element of eternal joy in it. Otherwise you will later receive ill will in return; or you will make people unhappy.

But I am boasting again!

In contrast, Gandhi's autobiography is one long confession that bears no trace of boasting – rather, it is like a transparent gem. By comparison, Rousseau's *Confessions*, which inspired a world-wide revolution, is bursting with passion. Someday I will have to write my confession, but it will be unbelievably ugly. For the present, I must settle for quickly finishing this book on young Gandhi while the boat is still docked in Rangoon. It is one o'clock in the morning, the 2nd of November. During the day it is so hot on ship and there is so much noise that it is difficult to write.

XII

Gandhi's Greatest Crime

A Father's Tears of Love

But much more serious than this theft was the one I was guilty of later. I pilfered the coppers when I was thirteen, possibly less. The other theft was committed when I was fifteen. In this case I stole a bit of gold out of my meat-eating brother's armlet. This brother had run into a debt of about twenty-five rupees. He had on his arm an armlet of solid gold. It was not difficult to clip a bit out of it.

Well, it was done, and the debt cleared. But this became more than I could bear. I resolved never to steal again. I also made up my mind to confess it to my father. But I did not dare to speak. Not that I was afraid of my father beating me. No. I do not recall his ever having beaten any of us. I was afraid of the pain that I should cause him. But I felt that the risk should be taken; that there could not be a cleansing without a clean confession.

I decided at last to write out the confession, to submit it to my father, and ask his forgiveness. I wrote it on a slip of paper and handed it to him myself. In this note, not only did I confess my guilt, but I also asked adequate punishment for it and closed with a request to him not to punish himself for my offence. I also pledged myself never to steal in the future.

I was trembling as I handed the confession to my father. He was suffering from a fistula and was confined in bed. His bed was a plain wooden plank. I handed him the note and sat opposite the plank.

He read it through, and pearl-drops trickled down his cheeks, wetting the paper. For a moment he closed his eyes in thought and then tore up the note. He had sat up to read it. He again lay down. I also cried. I could see my father's agony. If I were a painter I could draw a picture of the whole scene today. It is still so vivid in my mind.

Those pearl-drops of love cleansed my heart, and washed my sin away. Only he who has experienced such love can know what it is. As the hymn says:

> "Only he
> Who is smitten with the arrows of love,
> Knows its power." (pt. I, ch. VIII)

What a pure and touching soul this man had!

I had started to read this passage at one o'clock in the morning. And until dawn emotion prevented me from writing. My eyes were fixed on the text, but my pen remained immobile. Once before I had read this book and been so deeply touched that I spoke of it five or six times in my lectures. Now, with India so near, I am reading it again, all alone at night on the river at Rangoon. The tears are flowing, and my soul is filled with an exquisite tranquility. It is as though young Gandhi were right here before me.

On the boat there are hundreds of Hindus of all social classes. Their eyes are soft and kind. There are young boys and girls in simple native costumes accompanied by their noble-looking parents, and on the deck there are hundreds of poor passengers traveling fourth or fifth class. Writing this book under such circumstances, I am all the more pervaded by thoughts of young Gandhi.

Moreover, he reminds me of myself when, at the age of twenty, I arrived in Europe for the first time. In the following twenty years, always alone and fearful, I traveled through the countries of France, Germany, Spain, and England. Crossing over the Pyrenees into Basque country, the Republic of Andorra with a population of five thousand (the President at the time was a barber), I ended up in Elyzondo, a village of bandits. (Very pleasant and very hospitable, these bandits lodged me among them for a month without charge.)

Comparing these two youthful histories, I cannot tell if I am Gandhi or it is Gandhi that is me.

Mr. Maruyama did well to loan me Gandhi's book just before my departure for India. I had already written about Gandhi in magazines and books, but being extremely busy before my departure, I hadn't had time to give his book a thorough reading. Now I have begun reading without being able to stop.

The unexpected similarity I have found between Gandhi and myself has been a great joy to me. So, I am now even more captivated by the idea of writing the book on Gandhi than I had been prior to my departure. Mr. Maruyama had asked me several times if the manuscript were finished, and each time I had to tell him "no." And each time, right up to the day of departure, I renewed my resolve to write it. However, if I had done so, I would not be writing the book now, here on the river at Rangoon, under such special circumstances.

For Gandhi, his father's attitude was an unforgettable lesson.

This was, for me, an object-lesson in *Ahimsa* (literally "no-harm," or "non-violence"). Then, I could read in it nothing more than a father's love, but today I know that it was pure *Ahimsa*. When such *Ahimsa* becomes all-embracing, it transforms everything it touches. There is no limit to its power.

This sort of sublime forgiveness was not natural to my father. I had thought that he would be angry, say hard things, and strike his forehead. But he was so wonderfully peaceful, and I believe this was due to my clean confession. A clean confession, combined with a promise never to commit the sin again, when offered before one who has the right to receive it, is the purest type of repentance. I know that my confession made my father feel absolutely safe about me, and increased his affection for me beyond measure. (pt. I, ch. VIII)

The time of which I am now speaking is my sixteenth year. My father, as we have seen, was bedridden, suffering from a fistula. My mother, an old servant of the house, and I were his principal attendants. I had the duties of a nurse, which mainly consisted in dressing the wound, giving my father his medicine, and compounding drugs whenever they had to be made up at home. Every night I massaged his legs and retired only when he asked me to do so or after he had fallen asleep. I loved to do this service. I do not remember ever having neglected it. All the time at my disposal, after the performance of daily duties, was divided between school and attending on my father. I would only go out for an evening walk either when he permitted me or when he was feeling well. (pt. I, ch. IX)

Gandhi is so gentle, so tender!

Body and soul, he is gentleness and sweetness itself. How is it possible for one to have a soul like this? If only more people like this existed, all conflicts and crimes, all cares and evils would vanish from the face of the earth.

To be sure, such a soul is not the result of the daily instruction from the teachers at school, nor is it the result of the verbal education received from the parents. Rather it is the result of the conduct, attitudes and faith of the parents. The parents that are capable of encouraging the formation of such a soul in their children are those who embrace everything, including the sins and crimes of other people, who live every day sensing their own imperfection, pettiness, and ignorance, and with infinite humility.

XIII

Do You Not Lie?

Your Face Becomes Darker When You Lie

You say that you have never lied or stolen?
. . . Very well, but wouldn't you have stolen if you had found yourself in the same situation as Gandhi?
. . . Very well, but if you had been in the same situation as I, wouldn't you have stolen?
. . . Very well. Still, if for a long time you found yourself in the depths of a poverty that was even worse than mine – one in which you had nothing to eat or wear – wouldn't you steal? It would be very difficult not to steal, wouldn't it? I wouldn't blame you for stealing, nor do I think you should be punished by the authorities.

I can only say that theft is already punishment in itself – a great and frightful punishment from heaven. First of all, it causes you to lose your freedom and independence. Secondly, stealing causes you to lose the joy of all created things, the joy that causes you to feel kindness towards others and to be loved by others.

How sad life is when you cannot laugh from the bottom of your heart!

He who steals, fears that others will steal from him. Day and night he lives with the fear of being robbed. There is nothing

53

more painful than to live in constant suspicion of other people.

The world of doubt is the world of shadows. You can see nothing in there. The light of hope, the joyous dream is hidden by the shadows.

He who has enclosed himself in the black clouds of doubt experiences constant anxiety. Traveling alone and hesitantly through an endless territory in the blackness of night, he never knows when he will fall into a deep river or tread upon a poisonous snake.

Picture life in a world where everything is completely joyous, where there is nothing to detest, where everyone is a friend, a brother or a sister. Now picture a person with a suspicious mind entering into such a world. Can't you see that he would destroy it, transforming it into a hell of fear and anxiety?

Cinderella had exactly the opposite attitude towards life: She worked for her malicious stepmother just as she would have worked for her own affectionate mother. She bore no hatred towards her abominable stepsisters. And she maintained this attitude even though she was loaded down with hard, dirty work from morning until night. But because there was no doubt in her heart, she became very happy.

Cinderella entertained no doubts when the pumpkin became a coach and the mice became horses, when her soiled and tattered clothes turned into the beautiful robes of a princess, and even when the prince arrived to escort her to the ball. If her heart had been full of doubt, her stepmother and stepsisters would have become the incarnation of hatred for her. She would have suffered constantly.

When the heart is pervaded by doubt, the face becomes ugly and weak, the facial expression mean, the voice hysterical, and behavior inconsiderate. Even a beggar will not come near, let alone a prince. A heart as sweet and noble as the wildflowers is transformed by lies and theft into one that is hideous and corroded by doubt.

Does a more appalling punishment exist? Is there any conduct more detestable? Lying and stealing mar the most beautiful face with a veil of doubt. The most careful efforts to cover it with make-up are in vain. The eyes have lost their sparkle and tranquility and the disturbed heart is revealed for all to see.

My dear ladies and gentlemen, a woman should be the eternal incarnation of sweetness and beauty, and a man should be the eternal incarnation of courage and valor. Otherwise they can never be happy.

Beauty to women, courage to men. How regrettable it is when beauty and courage is replaced by ugliness and cowardice as a consequence of one theft or one lie.

Lying is a more frightful punishment than stealing. Stealing is a relatively petty sin that causes other people a certain amount of inconvenience, petty in comparison with lying. Lying, because it is the act of selling the soul to the devil, is far more serious. What is the exact relationship of lying to stealing? They are the spiritual and behavioral counterparts of one another. A liar cannot help but steal. Stealing is lying in action.

Included in the category of liars are those who are ungrateful, those who do not return what they borrow, those who are late for their appointments, those who renege on their promises, and, last but not least, those who cheat with time, who neglect their duties, and who are slow with their work.

XIV

Why Do People Lie?

Because They Have Brains

Above all, why do people lie? Why do they steal?

Because they have brains and are thus capable of thinking. Every animal that possesses such a brain lies. The thinking brain introduces intelligence. Those animals that do not possess such a brain do not lie. To be sure, dogs and cats often take their food by stealth, but this is not truly theft. It is their owners (who would otherwise strike them) that cause them to do this. It amounts to a conditioned reflex. Therefore, if they do not take food from man, it is not because they possess a moral judgment that prohibits such conduct.

Consequently, if it is through fear of punishment by the courts, the police, or the schoolmaster that you do not lie and steal, you are inferior to a dog or cat. You are inferior because you *do* have a conscious mind. Think about that for a while.

Many people do not lie and steal simply because they are afraid to. The resulting high opinion that they hold of themselves is ludicrous because, in reality, they are inferior to animals. In other words, even though they do not lie, they are liars. Although they are humans (or at least they have the face and form of humans), they do not have as much freedom as a dog or a cat.

57

Allow me to develop this theme in the form of an imaginary dialogue:

How does it happen that man has a brain?

It is man himself who created it. It is you who created it, and no one else.

Why was the brain created?

Because there was a need for it.

What was it needed for?

In order to lie.

Why is it necessary to lie in this life?

Because, without falsehoods, life wouldn't be very amusing.

Why is life without falsehoods not amusing?

April Fools' jokes are amusing, aren't they?

April Fool? That I don't understand at all.

Hmm, for a youngster you have the soul of a little old scholar. In fact, you remind me of a moralist or an ethics professor. . . . Let's suppose that there were no lies, falsehoods, or illusions in the world. Life would be as monotonous as a watch; life would be boring. If there were no falsehoods, there would be no tales, no stories, no adventure novels, love stories, or detective novels. Mickey Mouse, Popeye, Gulliver, Alice in Wonderland, Lincoln, Franklin, Buddha – all would disappear. All books would become dictionaries and texts on algebra, geometry, and law. There would be no more song, poetry, or haiku. And above all, there would be no more dreams – amusing, sad, frightening, and grandiose dreams – of an ideal and marvelous world. And, without a marvelous dream, there would be no joy in living. If the falsehood known as *dream* didn't exist, Lincoln, Edison, and Franklin would have committed suicide in childhood.

Then falsehoods and dreams are the same thing?

Exactly!

Then it's okay to lie?

No, that's not it either. But I will say that there is nothing so amusing as falsehood and theft.

What? Really!

Yes, it's true. You yourself stole milk from your mother the day after you were born.

But that was milk my mother gave to me. . . .

So what would have happened if she had refused to give it to you? You would have screamed as though you had been put into fire – waa, waa, waa. A baby threatening its mother is an act of violence. If you had been stronger and more intelligent when you were a baby, you would have stolen your milk. Another, better example: Haven't you stolen air since the day of your birth?

But air is everywhere.

That may be so, but it is not air that you created yourself. If a big department store were to offer its wares to you free, and you accepted them, wouldn't that be stealing?

Accepting them and stealing them is not the same thing. . . .

What is the difference between accepting and stealing? There isn't any. Just as soon as there is no law against taking things, you take them. You catch fish in the sea, and, when you feel like it, you capture crickets, grasshoppers, dragon flies, and butter-flies.

But aren't grasshoppers harmful insects?

Harmful? Who decided they were harmful? Man, wasn't it? If a grasshopper is a small harmful organism, then man is a big, harmful one. Surely the grasshoppers are angrily saying that it is man that is harmful, that it is man that is stealing their food from them. Moreover, during wars and famines, he sometimes eats them.

Then the whole world is harmful and threatening.

No, everyone is a liar. April Fool!

But isn't this what we call the "struggle for existence?"

That is still another falsehood. This life is infinitely amusing and joyful; it is not at all the terrible hell symbolized by the expression "struggle for existence." Did your mother ever think that you and your sisters and brothers would fight, that you would kill one another? If life were ruled by a "struggle for existence," that's what you would have done.

Well, where are we with this problem? . . . Bah, I understand nothing!

Wait, don't look so sad. I still maintain that this world is infinitely joyful and amusing, right to the very end. Allow me to explain why.

Because a world without falsehood would be as barren, mediocre, and sad as the face of an ethics professor, man created lies. For this he developed a machine called the "thinking brain." But because that world of falsehoods was not much fun either, man decided to discover that which isn't a lie, the Truth. Thus, he embarked upon a search for that which never changes, that which eternally stays the same – the Truth.

But this quest has turned out to be extremely difficult. For example, Sir Isaac Newton, due to his discovery of the laws of gravitation, has been considered the ultimate word in physics for over two hundred years. Nevertheless, he says, "I am like a child who is content with finding a few worthless seashells. Even though I reached the shore of the Ocean of Truth, I never put my foot into the water. I found only pretty shells on the beach."

Now, although Newton's law of gravitation is somewhat of a falsehood, his likening of it to a seashell is true. And this seashell is as commonplace as the ones you bought on that trip to the ocean when you were a grade school student. And still Newton became a great man, respected these many years. Now that it is your turn, will you dare to leap into that ocean called Truth?

Why not? For this leap, you have no need of money, knowledge, entrance exams, or special qualifications. You don't even need clothes or shoes. You can plunge in stark naked, it will still be okay. The elite of the world – all those professors and students at the Universities and Institutes – are only searching for seashells on the beach. In their lifetimes they will only discover two or three.

Fortunately, and contrary to what most people think, the way is really not very rough or thorny. So why not, like Gandhi, make a plunge into the Ocean of Truth?

The relative world is the world of falsehood; there it is very difficult to find true happiness and joy. Therefore, if you do find them in the relative world, joy and happiness are even greater.

In Gandhi's country, this world of falsehoods and illusions is known as *Maya*. Without exception, everything pertaining to this world soon vanishes without a trace, like foam on the waves. A relative happiness gotten through great effort is of little value because it disappears in an instant. It is like the treasure you find in your dream that vanishes upon awakening. It is in vain to accumulate a hundred or a thousand illusory joys of this kind. Better to find one that will never disappear: The Truth.

Another name for this is the Order of the Universe. It has one law which is called the Unique Principle.

However, in spite of my explanations I know that the world does not appear to you as an ephemeral dream. This is quite natural. It is something that can only be understood when you reach the level of Newton. No matter, I will continue my exposition.

We believe in the existence of everything that we can see,

hear, touch, smell, and taste. But, in reality, that belief is a falsehood. Our experience may be compared with viewing television. We are satisfied with watching it, but the images are *Maya*; there is nothing in the television set. The images are composed simply of ordinary electromagnetic waves that are found everywhere in the universe. These waves you cannot see or hear. Taste, form, smell, color, and sound are all electromagnetic waves, too. When you capture these waves with your senses they become real for you, just as the waves captured by the television apparatus become images. Although electromagnetic waves are universally and eternally present, they rapidly disappear in our sensual world; and thus Gandhi, Franklin, and Lincoln have disappeared. Even yesterday's dinner has already disappeared. Everything takes on the character of a dream, an illusion.

Young Gandhi, the perfect example of purity and sweetness, where is he now?

Only he who finds in this world of lies and illusion the Truth of the Order of the Universe that never disappears can realize Eternal Happiness, Infinite Freedom, and Absolute Justice. In this infinite Ocean of Truth, he will find millions of beautiful and mysterious seashells – not the dead shells of Newton.

Gandhi, it is Gandhi.

You, it is you.

Gandhi is you, and you are Gandhi – Gandhi and you are identical. The proof is that you love Gandhi. To love means to understand. To understand means to be alike.

If everything in the world originates in electromagnetic waves, then your form and shadow are a materialization of those waves. Gandhi is another such shadow and form. Thus, you and Gandhi have the same origin. This is, of course, not limited to Gandhi: Franklin as well as Lincoln, the stars as well as the sun, the infinite blue sky above you, for all that, the entire universe is nothing but you.

It is now 4:00 a.m., the 3rd of November, 1953. Without stop I have been writing this passage since 2:00 a.m. in the splendid, first-class library of the packet boat *Sadhana*, still docked at Rangoon. There has been an agreeable breeze made by three big electric fans. The boat leaves port on the 6th, and then makes another call at Akiabe, occupied by the Japanese just a few years ago. Then, it is on to Calcutta. Finally I will be in Gandhi's country of birth.

Yesterday we were overwhelmed by an invasion of grasshoppers. There are still quite a few survivors in this room. One is on my table, so tranquil that it does not try to get away when I touch it. My dear grasshopper, are you not a reincarnation of Gandhi?

Up on the darkened deck of the ship, many people are sleeping. These are the Hindu deck passengers.

Above them in the heavens the stars are shining. Every one of those stars is our past and our future. And the whole of that is our soul.

XV

Thoughts of a Sixteen-Year-Old Boy

Searching for the Truth

Gandhi, the crybaby, the child with the weak and timid spirit, reached the age of sixteen. Inspired by the reading of various books, he began to ponder questions about nature, the universe, life, and human destiny. He posed questions to every kind of person he met without receiving answers that satisfied him. At this time he was still not acquainted with the philosophy of *Ahimsa*. Although he had given up the carnivorous diet, Gandhi was still not deeply convinced that, for him, that type of diet, more than being merely harmful, was a sin.

Thus, he entered into adolescence. Although his philosophy of life was still not well-defined, he had begun to have some vague ideas about the path he should take. This can be seen in the following words:

> But one thing took deep root in me – the conviction that morality is the basis of things, and that truth is the substance of all morality. Truth became my sole objective. It began to grow in magnitude every day, and my definition of it also has been ever widening.
>
> A Gujarati didactic stanza likewise gripped my mind and heart. Its precept – return good for evil – became my guiding principle. It became such a passion

that I began numerous experiments in it. Here are
those (for me) wonderful lines:

> "For a bowl of water give a goodly meal;
> For a kindly greeting bow thou down with zeal;
> For a simple penny pay thou back with gold;
> If thy life be rescued, life do not withhold.
> Thus the words and actions of the wise regard;
> Every little service tenfold they reward.
> But the truly noble know all men as one,
> And return with gladness good for evil done."
> (pt. I, ch. X)

This is the heart of the Buddhist saying, "From one grain,
ten thousand." One grain of rice gives ten thousand at the
harvest: That is the way of nature. The way to enter into the
world of Happiness and Freedom is to return the joy you have
received multiplied many times over.

How admirable is the phrase, "But the truly noble know all
men as one." Do you know a boy or girl who thinks that deeply
at the age of sixteen? Do you have, my dear reader, a philosophy as profound? Already, at the age of sixteen, Gandhi had
decided the direction of his life. And he put it into practice. He
who speaks the truth gives supreme judgment to others; consequently, he is giving them the greatest freedom of action. This
is the highest goal of the way of life I have been describing.

Gandhi's life was consecrated entirely to finding and assimi-
lating the Truth. Still, he did not fully understand what Truth
was during his adolescence. He was still only a boy, little different from others. What eventually caused him to tower above
the rest of humanity is that he never gave up his ardent quest
for the Truth until the moment of his death.

XVI

The Student Period

Vows of Vegetarianism and Abstinence

Married at the age of thirteen and having to repeat a grade in school, Gandhi was far from being a brilliant student. Nonetheless, his parents insisted that he attend a university. He finally departed for school in England, but he had many difficulties to surmount before he was able to do this. These difficulties serve as good examples of the unvarying rules of the world: "After sorrow comes joy." "The bigger the front, the bigger the back." "Yang comes after yin." Let us follow his experiences to see how a young man was courageously able to overcome the difficulties that relentlessly fell upon him:

> My elders wanted me to pursue my studies at college after the matriculation. There was a college in Bhavnagar as well as in Bombay, and as the former was cheaper, I decided to go there and join the Samaldas College. I went, but found myself entirely at sea. Everything was difficult. I could not follow, let alone take an interest in, the professors' lectures. It was no fault of theirs. The professors in that College were regarded as first-rate. But I was so raw. At the end of the first term, I returned home.
>
> We had in Mavji Dave, who was a shrewd and

learned Brahman, an old friend and adviser of the family.
. . . Learning that I was at Samaldas College, he said:
"The times are changed. And none of you can expect
to succeed to your father's *gadi* without having had a
proper education. Now as this boy is still pursuing his
studies, you should all look to him to keep the *gadi*. It
will take him four or five years to get his B.A. degree,
which will at best qualify him for a sixty rupees' post,
not for a Diwanship. If like my son he went in for
law, it would take him still longer, by which time
there would be a host of lawyers aspiring for a Diwan's post. I would far rather that you sent him to
England. My son Kevalram says it is very easy to
become a barrister. In three years' time he will return.
Also expenses will not exceed four to five thousand
rupees. . . ."

Joshiji – that is how we used to call old Mavji Dave
– turned to me with complete assurance, and asked:
"Would you not rather go to England than study
here?" Nothing could have been more welcome to
me. I was fighting shy of my difficult studies. So I
jumped at the proposal and said that the sooner I was
sent the better. It was no easy business to pass exami-
nations quickly. Could I not be sent to qualify for the
medical profession?

My brother interrupted me: "Father never liked it.
He had you in mind when he said that we Vaishnavas
should have nothing to do with dissection of dead
bodies. Father intended you for the bar."

Joshiji chimed in: "I am not opposed to the medical profession as was Gandhiji. Our *Shastras* are not
against it. But a medical degree will not make a Diwan
of you, and I want you to be Diwan, or if possible
something better. Only in that way could you take

under your protecting care your large family. The times are fast changing and getting harder every day. It is the wisest thing therefore to become a barrister.
. . ."

My elder brother was greatly exercised in his mind. How was he to find the wherewithal to send me? And was it proper to trust a young man like me to go abroad alone?

My mother was sorely perplexed. She did not like the idea of parting with me. This is how she tried to put me off: "Uncle," she said, "is the eldest member of the family. He should first be consulted. If he consents we will consider the matter. . . ."

I arrived at last, did obeisance to my uncle, and told him everything. He thought it over and said: "I am not sure whether it is possible for one to stay in England without prejudice to one's own religion. From all I have heard, I have my doubts. When I meet these big barristers, I see no difference between their life and that of the Europeans. They know no scruples regarding food. Cigars are never out of their mouths. They dress as shamelessly as Englishmen. All that would not be in keeping with our family tradition. I am shortly going on a pilgrimage and have not many years to live. At the threshold of death, how dare I give you permission to go to England, to cross the seas? But I will not stand in your way. It is your mother's permission which really matters. If she permits you, then godspeed! Tell her I will not interfere. You will go with my blessings. . . ."

My mother, however, was still unwilling. She had begun making minute inquiries. Someone had told her that young men got lost in England. Someone else had said that they took to meat; and yet another that they could not live there without liquor. "How about all this?" she asked me. I said, "Will you not trust me? I shall not lie to you. I swear that I shall not touch any of those things. If there were any such danger, would Joshiji let me go?"

"I can trust you," she said. "But how can I trust you in a distant land? I am dazed and know not what to do. I will ask Becharji Swami."

Becharji Swami was originally a Modh Bania, but had now become a Jain monk. He too was a family adviser like Joshiji. He came to my help, and said: "I shall get the boy solemnly to take the three vows, and then he can be allowed to go." He administered the oath and I vowed not to touch wine, woman and meat. This done, my mother gave her permission. . . . (pt. I, ch. XI)

With my mother's permission and blessings, I set off exultantly for Bombay, leaving my wife with a baby of a few months. But on arrival there, friends told my brother that the Indian Ocean was rough in June and July, and as this was my first voyage, I should not be allowed to sail until November. Someone also reported that a steamer had just been sunk in a gale. This made my brother uneasy, and he refused to take the risk of allowing me to sail immediately. . . .

Meanwhile, my caste-people were agitated over my going abroad. No Modh Bania had been to England up to now, and if I dared to do so, I ought to be brought to book! A general meeting of the caste was called and I was summoned to appear before it. I went. How I managed to muster up the courage I do not know. Nothing daunted, and without the slightest hesitation, I came before the meeting. The Sheth – the headman of the community – who was distantly related to me and had been on very good terms with my father, thus accosted me:

"In the opinion of the caste, your proposal to go to England is not proper. Our religion forbids voyages abroad. We have also heard that it is not possible to live there without compromising our religion. One is obliged to eat and drink with the Europeans!"

To which I replied: "I do not think that it is at all against our religion to go to England. I intend going there for further studies. And I have already solemnly promised to my mother to abstain from three things you fear most. I am sure the vow will keep me safe."

"But we tell you," rejoined the Sheth, "that it is *not* possible to keep our religion there. You know my relations with your father and you ought to listen to my advice."

"I know those relations," said I. "And you are as an elder to me. But I am helpless in this matter. I cannot alter my resolve to go to England. My father's friend and adviser, who is a learned Brahman, sees no objection to my going to England, and my mother and brother have also given me their permission."

"But will you disregard the orders of the caste?"

"I am really helpless. I think the caste should not interfere in the matter."

This incensed the Sheth. He swore at me. I sat unmoved. So the Sheth pronounced his order: "This boy shall be treated as an outcaste from today. Whoever helps him or goes to see him off at the dock shall be punishable with a fine of one rupee four annas. . . ."

The incident, however, made me more anxious than ever to sail. What would happen if they succeeded in bringing pressure to bear on my brother?

Supposing something unforeseen happened? As I was thus worrying over my predicament, I heard that a Junagadh vakil was going to England, for being called to the bar, by a boat sailing on the 4th of September. I met the friends to whose care my brother had commended me. They also agreed that I should not let go the opportunity of going in such company. There was no time to be lost. I wired to my brother for permission, which he granted. I asked my brother-in-law to give me the money. But he referred to the order of the Sheth and said that he could not afford to lose caste. I then sought a friend of the family and requested him to accommodate me to the extent of my passage and sundries, and to recover the loan from my brother. The friend was not only good enough to accede to my request, but he cheered me up as well. I was so thankful. With part of the money I at once purchased the passage. Then I had to equip myself for the voyage. . . . A berth was reserved for me by my friends in the same cabin as that of Sjt. Tryambakrai Mazmudar, the Junagadh vakil. They also commended me to him. He was an experienced man of mature age and knew the world. I was yet a stripling of eighteen without any experience of the world. Sjt. Mazmudar told my friends not to worry about me.

I sailed at last from Bombay on the 4th of September. . . . (pt. I, ch. XII)

We reached Southampton, as far as I remember, on a Saturday. On the boat I had worn a black suit, the white flannel one, which my friends had got me, having been kept especially for wearing when I landed. I had thought that white clothes would suit me better when I stepped ashore, and therefore I did so in white flannels. Those were the last days of September, and I

found I was the only person wearing such clothes.
. . . The shame of being the only person in white
clothes was already too much for me. . . .

I would continually think of my home and country.
My mother's love always haunted me. At night the
tears would stream down my cheeks, and home
memories of all sorts made sleep out of the question.
It was impossible to share my misery with anyone.
And even if I could have done so, where was the use?
I knew of nothing that would soothe me. Everything
was strange – the people, their ways, and even their
dwellings. I was a complete novice in the matter of
English etiquette and continually had to be on my
guard. There was the additional inconvenience of the
vegetarian vow. Even the dishes that I could eat were
tasteless and insipid. I thus found myself between
Scylla and Charybdis. England I could not bear, but to
return to India was not to be thought of. Now that I
had come, I must finish the three years, said the inner
voice. (pt. I, ch XIII)

XVII

The English Life

Some Experiments That Failed

Doctor Mehta, a Hindu well-known in London, was a truly kind and gracious man, even though he was living among the very people who for 150 years had enslaved and violently exploited India. What pain, what difficulties he must have suffered in order to attain his position.

One day as Doctor Mehta was inspecting the house, the room, and the furniture where Gandhi was living, he shook his head. "This place won't do," he said. "We come to England not so much for the purpose of studies as for gaining experience of English life and customs. And for this you need to live with a family. But before you do so, I think you had better serve a period of apprenticeship with N. I will take you there." (pt. I, ch. XIV)

Gandhi moved to N.'s boarding house where the problem soon became the food. Although the landlady was cordial and helpful to him, he could not stand the raw salads and the vegetables boiled in water without seasoning. He tried to fill his stomach solely with oatmeal at breakfast, and boiled spinach and two or three slices of bread with jam at lunch and dinner. But his stomach did not easily fill up on such light fare. Still, thinking it would be impolite, he was ashamed to ask for more than two or three slices of bread.

His friend, N., constantly pushed him towards meat, but Gandhi desperately defended his vow.

> The friend once got disgusted with this state of things, and said: "Had you been my own brother, I would have sent you packing. What is the value of a vow made before an illiterate mother, and in ignorance of conditions here? It is no vow at all. It would not be regarded as a vow in law. It is pure superstition to stick to such a promise. And I tell you this persistence will not help you to gain anything here. You confess to having eaten and relished meat. You took it where it was absolutely unnecessary, and will not take it where it is essential. What a pity!"
>
> But I was adamant.
>
> Day in and day out the friend would argue, but I had an eternal negative to face him with. The more he argued, the more uncompromising I became. Daily I would pray for God's protection and get it. Not that I had any idea of God. It was faith that was at work – faith of which the seed had been sown by the good nurse Rambha. . . .
>
> During [my] wanderings I once hit on a vegetarian restaurant in Farringdon Street. The sight of it filled me with the same joy that a child feels on getting a thing after its own heart. Before I entered I noticed books for sale under a glass window near the door. I saw among them Salt's *Plea for Vegetarianism*. This I purchased for a shilling and went straight to the dining room. This was my first hearty meal since my arrival in England. God had come to my aid.
>
> I read Salt's book from cover to cover and was much impressed by it. From the date of reading this

book, I may claim to have become a vegetarian by choice. I blessed the day on which I had taken the vow before my mother. I had all along abstained from meat in the interest of truth and of the vow I had taken, but had wished at the same time that every Indian should be a meat-eater, and had looked forward to being one myself freely and openly some day, and to enlisting others in the cause. The choice was now made in favor of vegetarianism, the spread of which henceforward became my mission. (pt. I, ch. XIV)

. . . The clothes after the Bombay cut that I was wearing were, I thought, unsuitable for English society, and I got new ones at the Army and Navy Stores. I also went in for a chimney-pot hat costing nineteen shillings – an excessive price in those days. Not content with this, I wasted ten pounds on an evening suit made in Bond Street, the centre of fashionable life in London; and got my good and noble-hearted brother to send me a double watch-chain of gold. It was not correct to wear a ready-made tie and I learnt the art of tying one for myself. While in India, the mirror had been a luxury permitted on the days when the family barber gave me a shave. Here I wasted ten minutes every day before a huge mirror, watching myself arranging my tie and parting my hair in the correct fashion. . . .

As if all this were not enough to make me look the thing, I directed my attention to other details that were supposed to go towards the making of an English gentleman. I was told that it was necessary for me to take lessons in dancing, French, and elocution. . . . I decided to take dancing lessons at a class and paid down three pounds as fees for a term. I must have taken about six lessons in three weeks. But it was beyond me to achieve anything like rhythmic motion. I could not follow the piano and hence found it impossible to keep time. What then was I to do? The recluse in the fable kept a cat to keep off the rats, and then a cow to feed the cat with milk, and a man to keep the cow and so on. My ambitions also grew like the family of the recluse. I thought I should learn to play the violin in order to cultivate an ear for Western music. So I invested three pounds in a violin and something more in fees. I sought a third teacher to give me lessons in elocution and paid him a preliminary fee of a guinea. He recommended Bell's *Standard Elocutionist* as the textbook, which I purchased. . . .

But Mr. Bell rang the bell of alarm in my ear and I awoke.

I had not to spend a lifetime in England, I said to myself. What then was the use of learning elocution? And how could dancing make a gentleman of me? The violin I could learn even in India. I was a student and ought to go on with my studies. I should qualify myself to join the Inns of Court. If my character made a gentleman of me, so much the better. Otherwise I should forego the ambition.

These and similar thoughts possessed me, and I expressed them in a letter to the elocution teacher, requesting him to excuse me from further lessons. I had taken only two or three. I wrote a similar letter to the dancing teacher, and went personally to the violin teacher with a request to dispose of the violin for any price it might fetch. She was rather friendly to me, so I told her how I had discovered that I was pursuing a false idea. She encouraged me in the determination to make a complete change.

This infatuation must have lasted about three months. The punctiliousness in dress persisted for years. But henceforward I became a student. (pt. I, ch. XV)

Let no one imagine that my experiments in dancing and the like marked a stage of indulgence in my life. The reader will have noticed that even then I had my wits about me. That period of infatuation was not unrelieved by a certain amount of self-introspection on my part. I kept account of every farthing I spent, and my expenses were carefully calculated. . . .

As I kept strict watch over my way of living, I could see that it was necessary to economize. I therefore decided to reduce my expenses by half. My accounts showed numerous items spent on fares. Again my living with a family meant the payment of a regular weekly bill. It also included the courtesy of occasionally taking members of the family out to dinner, and likewise attending parties with them. All this involved heavy items for conveyances, especially as, if the friend was a lady, custom required that the man should pay all the expenses. Also dining out meant extra cost, as no deduction could be made from the regular weekly bill for meals not taken. It seemed to me that all these items should be saved, as likewise the drain on my purse caused through a false sense of propriety.

So I decided to take rooms on my own account, instead of living any longer in a family, and also to remove from place to place according to the work I had to do, thus gaining experience at the same time. The rooms were so selected as to enable me to reach the place of business on foot in half an hour, and so save fares. Before this I had always taken some kind of conveyance whenever I went anywhere, and had to find extra time for walks. The new arrangement combined walks and economy, as it meant a saving of fares and gave me walks that kept me practically free from illness throughout my stay in England and gave me a fairly strong body. . . .

I also came across books on simple living. I gave up the suite of rooms and rented one instead, invested in a stove, and began cooking my breakfast at home. The process scarcely took me more than twenty minutes for there was only oatmeal porridge to cook and water to boil for cocoa. I had lunch out and for dinner bread and cocoa at home. Thus I managed to live on a shilling and three pence a day. This was also a period of intensive study. Plain living saved me plenty of time and I passed my examination.

Let not the reader think that this living made my life by any means a dreary affair. On the contrary the change harmonized my inward and outward life. It was also more in keeping with the means of my family. My life was certainly more truthful and my soul knew no bounds of joy. (pt. I, ch. XVI)

There were comparatively few Indian students in England forty years ago. It was a practice among them to affect the bachelor even though they might be married. School or college students in England are all bachelors, studies being regarded as incompatible with married life. We had that tradition in the good old days, a student then being known as a *bramachari* [practitioner of *bramacharya*, or chastity]. But in these days we have child-marriages, a thing practically unknown in England. Indian youths in England, therefore, felt ashamed to confess that they were married. There was also another reason for dissembling, namely that in event of the fact being known it would be impossible for the young men to go about or flirt with the young girls of the family in which they lived. The flirting was more or less innocent. Parents even encouraged it; and that sort of association between young men and young women may even be a necessity there, in view of the fact that every young man has to choose his mate. If, however, Indian youths on arrival in England indulge in these relations, quite natural to English youths, the result is likely to be disastrous, as has often been found. I saw that our youths had succumbed to the temptation and chosen a life of untruth for the sake of companionships which, however innocent in the case of English youths, were for them undesirable. I too caught the contagion. I did not hesitate to pass myself off as a bachelor though I was married and the father of a son. But I was none the happier for being a dissembler. . . .

It was customary in families like the one in which I was staying at Ventnor for the daughter of the landlady to take out guests for a walk. My landlord's daughter took me one day to the lovely hills round Ventnor. I was no slow walker, but my companion walked even faster, dragging me after her and chattering all the while. I responded to her chatter sometimes with a whispered "yes" or "no," or at the most "yes, how beautiful!" She was flying like a bird whilst I was wondering when I should get back home. We thus reached the top of a hill. How to get down again was the question. In spite of her high-heeled boots this sprightly young lady of twenty-five darted down the hill like an arrow. I was shamefacedly struggling to get down. She stood at the foot smiling and cheering me and offering to come and drag me. How could I be so chicken-hearted? With the greatest difficulty, and crawling at intervals, I somehow managed to scramble to the bottom. She loudly laughed "bravo" and shamed me all the more, as well she might.

But I could not escape scatheless everywhere. For God wanted to rid me of the canker of untruth. (pt. I, ch. XIX)

XVIII

Young Gandhi
and English Girls

Sensuality Veils Truth and Justice

The young English girls were so impishly beguiling that amo-
rous temptations soon assailed Gandhi: the girl at his boarding
house, the widow he met in the hotel restaurant with her affectionate invitations, the young ladies that lived with her, and so
forth.

Gandhi became so taken with one of these young ladies that
he almost became engaged to her, thus putting himself in a very
difficult position. Finally, he could no longer stand the falsehood he had created in not forewarning her that he was already
married. One day, in a long letter to the widow, he admitted the
truth. Here is his exquisitely original letter:

> "Ever since we met at Brighton you have been kind to
> me. You have taken care of me even as a mother of
> her son. You also think that I should be married and
> with that view you have been introducing me to young
> ladies. Rather than allow matters to go further, I must
> confess to you that I have been unworthy of your
> affection. I should have told you when I began my
> visits to you that I was married. I knew that Indian
> students in England dissembled the fact of their mar-
> riage and I followed suit. I now see that I should not

> have done so. I must also add that I was married while yet a boy, and am the father of a son. I am pained that I should have kept this knowledge from you so long. But I am glad God has now given me the courage to speak the truth. Will you forgive me? I assure you I have taken no improper liberties with the young lady you were good enough to introduce to me. I knew my limits. You, not knowing that I was married, naturally desired that we should be engaged. In order that things should not go beyond the present stage, I must tell you the truth.
>
> "If on receipt of this, you feel that I have been unworthy of your hospitality, I assure you I shall not take it amiss. You have laid me under such an everlasting debt of gratitude by your kindness and solicitude. If, after this, you do not reject me but continue to regard me as worthy of your hospitality, which I will spare no pains to deserve, I shall naturally be happy and count it a further token of your kindness."
> (pt. I, ch. XIX)

Gandhi experienced a great deal of discomfort while writing this letter, sometimes blushing, sometimes turning pale. He sent it off and almost by return post received an answer. The response is also noteworthy. In it, it can be seen that the English do not have the same moral attitude towards sex as do the inhabitants of the Far East. The English are light, generous, and rather negligent when it comes to sex. (When it comes to money and finances, however, they are very rigid and demanding.)

Here is the lady's reply:

> "I have your frank letter. We were both very glad and had a hearty laugh over it. The untruth you say you

have been guilty of is pardonable. But it is well that you have acquainted us with the real state of things. My invitation still stands and we shall certainly expect you next Sunday and look forward to hearing all about your child-marriage and to the pleasure of laughing at your expense. Need I assure you that our friendship is not in the least affected by this incident?" (pt. I, ch. XIX)

In spite of other, similar problems, Gandhi was able to preserve his traditional Far-Eastern concept of chastity in a society where the attitude towards sexual matters was radically different.

In contrast, how sad it is to see the increase in the numbers of young people who, especially after the war, are violating sexual order. By thus drowning themselves in sexual pleasure, they run the risk of ruining their lives. For them the great dreams of life soon disappear, for sensuality is even a more potent force in the veiling of high judgment than is sentimentality.

In the person who takes the path of pleasure through sensuality, desire progressively grows. For the senses are the engine that powers the world of illusion. Or rather, it is through them that we mistake the world of illusion for the world of truth. And, as desire becomes proportionately greater, it is transformed into violent passion. Then it catches fire and becomes blind violence. The heart gives up its quest for the ideal and high judgment is obliterated by passion.

No more will, no more soul, no more life!

XIX

The Discovery of the Far East

Leaving Home to Find It

It may seem curious, but a Japanese discovers more about his country and its people when he travels far away from Japan. If you do not go away from your home, you cannot understand what your home is. Your neighbor's flowers seem prettier, the happiness of other people is more apparent to you than your own. You do not truly know yourself because you lack perspective. For that same reason you cannot truly understand and appreciate your own country until you leave it.

Thus it was that Gandhi discovered the Far East for the first time while in London.

Towards the end of his second year there he found some genuinely exceptional friends. It would seem that an Easterner hasn't really understood the West no matter how long he has lived there until he has made friends of this kind. These two English friends were involved in reading a translation of the *Bhagavadgita*, a Sanskrit poem. This transcendental poem is comparable to the Japanese *Kojiki,* or to the *Norito.* Gandhi had never read the most inspired religious work of his own country! (A similar situation prevails in Japan where those that are known as "scholars" are for the most part those who study only Western thought.)

87

Overcome with shame, Gandhi began to read the *Bhagavad-gita* in Sanskrit along with his two friends.

> The book struck me as one of priceless worth. The impression has ever since been growing on me with the result that I regard it today as the book *par excellence* for the knowledge of Truth. It has afforded me invaluable help in my moments of gloom. I have read almost all the English translations of it, and I regard Sir Edwin Arnold's as the best. He has been faithful to the text and yet it does not read like a translation. Though I read the *Gita* with these two friends, I cannot pretend to have studied it then. It was only after some years that it became a book of daily reading.
>
> The two brothers also recommended *The Light of Asia* by Sir Edwin Arnold, whom I knew till then as the author only of *The Song Celestial*, and I read it with even greater interest than I did the *Bhagavad-gita*. Once I had begun it I could not leave off. (pt. I, ch. XX)

It was in this way that Gandhi discovered the Far East.

Not long afterwards he made another friend, a Christian and a vegetarian who did not smoke or drink. As he was an enthusiast of the Bible, he procured a copy for Gandhi.

Gandhi set himself to reading the Old Testament. He was able to finish the Book of Genesis, but the following sections he found to be boring. Only the Sermon on the Mount showed him that same spirit of renunciation that he had found in the *Bhagavadgita* and in *The Light of Asia*.

> But the New Testament produced a different impression, especially the Sermon on the Mount which went straight to my heart. I compared it with the *Gita*. The verses, "But I say unto you, that ye resist not evil: but

whosoever shall smite thee on thy right cheek, turn to him the other also. And if any man take away thy coat let him have thy cloak too," delighted me beyond measure and put me in mind of Shamal Bhatt's "For a bowl of water, give a goodly meal," etc. My young mind tried to unify the teaching of the *Gita, The Light of Asia* and the Sermon on the Mount. That renunciation was the highest form of religion appealed to me greatly. (pt. I, ch. XX)

As the idea of renunciation began to exercise a growing effect on him, he began to study the lives of the great masters of religion. In Carlyle's *Heroes and Hero-Worship*, he read the chapter on the hero as a prophet and learned of the prophet's greatness, courage, and austere living.

Beyond this acquaintance with religion I could not go at the moment, as reading for the examination left me scarcely any time for outside subjects. But I took mental note of the fact that I should read more religious books and acquaint myself with all the principal religions. (pt. I, ch. XX)

Gandhi's vision of the Far East increased in proportion to his reading. Many people waste this opportunity – an opportunity that comes only once in a lifetime.

XX

A World Traveler in Indian Costume

An Eccentric Friend

Around this time a curious personage appeared in the life of Gandhi, Narayan Hemchandra, a Hindu.

Narayan Hemchandra did not speak English. Moreover, he dressed bizarrely. He wore wide pants, a Parsi-style brown overcoat, all wrinkled and dirty, no tie, no collar, and a wool hat with a tassel. To top it off he wore a full beard. Such a strange and curiously dressed person could not pass unnoticed in fashionable circles.

> We met daily. There was a considerable amount of similarity between our thoughts and actions. Both of us were vegetarians. We would often have our lunch together. This was the time when I lived on 17 shillings a week and cooked for myself. Sometimes I would go to his room, and sometimes he would come to mine. I cooked in the English style. Nothing but Indian style would satisfy him. He could not do without *dal*. I would make soup of carrots, etc., and he would pity me for my taste. Once he somehow hunted out *mung*, cooked it and brought it to my place. I ate it with delight. This led on to a regular system of exchange between us. I would take my delicacies to him and he would bring his to me.

91

Cardinal Manning's name was then on every lip. The dock labourers' strike had come to an early termination owing to the efforts of John Burns and Cardinal Manning. I told Narayan Hemchandra of Disraeli's tribute to the Cardinal's simplicity. "Then I must see the sage," said he.

"He is a big man. How do you expect to meet him?"

"Why? I know how. I must get you to write to him in my name. Tell him that I am an author and that I want to congratulate him personally on his humanitarian work, and also say that I shall have to take you as my interpreter as I do not know English."

I wrote a letter to that effect. In two or three days came Cardinal Manning's card in reply giving us an appointment. So we both called on the Cardinal. I put on the usual visiting suit. Narayan Hemchandra was the same as ever, in the same coat and the same trousers. I tried to make fun of this, but he laughed me out and said: "You civilized fellows are all cowards. Great men never look at a person's exterior. They think of his heart."

We entered the Cardinal's mansion. As soon as we were seated, a thin, tall, old gentleman made his appearance, and shook hands with us. Narayan Hemchandra thus gave his greetings:

"I do not want to take up your time. I had heard a lot about you and I felt I should come and thank you for the good work you have done for the strikers. It has been my custom to visit the sages of the world and that is why I have put you to this trouble."

This was of course my translation of what he spoke in Gujarati.

"I am glad you have come. I hope your stay in

London will agree with you and that you will get in touch with people here. God bless you."

With these words the Cardinal stood up and said good-bye. (pt. I, ch. XXII)

What a cheerful and jolly fellow Narayan is! He is exactly the opposite of Gandhi. Without money and without knowing English, he travels the world. This is an example of a young man who is yang. There are many young people of this kind in India and China: Vivekananda, Kou-Fou-Minh, Lin Yu-Tang, Tagore, etc. From Japan there is only one, Tenshin Okakura. There are, however, quite a few Japanese in the West who make their living by painting. Still, they have their painting technique as baggage, while Okakura, Narayan, and I set forth with only a philosophy, an idea. There is a considerable difference.

Once Narayan Hemchandra came to my place in a shirt and *dhoti*. The good landlady opened the door, came running to me in fright – this was a new landlady who did not know Narayan Hemchandra – and said: "A sort of madcap wants to see you." I went to the door and to my surprise found Narayan Hemchandra. I was shocked. His face, however, showed nothing but his usual smile.

"But did not the children in the street rag you?"

"Well, they ran after me, but I did not mind them and they were quiet."

Narayan Hemchandra went to Paris after a few months' stay in London. He began studying French and also translating French books. I knew enough French to revise his translation, so he gave it to me to read. It was not a translation, it was the substance.

Finally he carried out his determination to visit America. It was with great difficulty that he succeeded in securing a deck ticket. While in the United States he was prosecuted for "being indecently dressed," as he once went out in a shirt and *dhoti*. I have a recollection that he was discharged. (pt. I, ch. XXII)

Later, Gandhi was to travel everywhere in the civilized world – wearing nothing but a *dhoti* himself.

XXI

That Which You Also Have

Another Friend's Good Advice

At last Gandhi graduated from the university. But now, how was he to orient his life?

The following passages show that he had become extremely indecisive and yin due to the vegetarian diet that he had been following for three years in London.

> It was easy to be called, but it was difficult to practise at the bar. I had read the laws, but not learnt how to practise law. I had read with interest "Legal Maxims," but did not know how to apply them in my profession. . . .
>
> I was torn with these doubts and anxieties whilst I was studying law. I confided my difficulties to some of my friends. One of them suggested that I should seek Dadabhai Naoroji's advice. I have already said that when I went to England, I possessed a note of introduction to Dadabhai. I availed myself of it very late. I thought I had no right to trouble such a great man for an interview. Whenever an address by him was announced, I would attend it, listen to him from a corner of the hall, and go away after having feasted my eyes and ears. In order to come in close touch with the students he had founded an association. I used to attend

> its meetings, and rejoiced at Dadabhai's solicitude for the students, and the latter's respect for him. In course of time I mustered up courage to present to him the note of introduction. He said: "You can come and have my advice whenever you like." But I never availed myself of his offer. I thought it wrong to trouble him without the most pressing necessity. (pt. I, ch. XXV)

Can you see how timid and yin Gandhi had become? The following should convince you even more:

> I forget now whether it was the same friend or someone else who recommended me to meet Mr. Frederick Pincutt. He was Conservative, but his affection for the Indian students was pure and unselfish. Many students sought his advice and I also applied to him for an appointment, which he granted. I can never forget that interview. He greeted me as a friend. He laughed away my pessimism. "Do you think," he said, "that everyone must be Pherozeshah Mehta? Pherozeshahs and Badruddins are rare. Rest assured it takes no unusual skill to be an ordinary lawyer. Common honesty and industry are enough to enable him to make a living. All cases are not complicated. Well, let me know the extent of your general reading."
>
> When I acquainted him with my little stock of knowledge, he was, as I could see, rather disappointed. But it was only for a moment. Soon his face beamed with a pleasing smile and he said, "I understand your trouble. Your general reading is meagre. You have no knowledge of the world, a *sine qua non* for a vakil. You have not even read the history of India. A vakil should know human nature. He should be able to read a man's character from his face. And every Indian ought to know Indian history. This has

no connection with the practice of law, but you ought to have that knowledge. I see that you have not even read Kaye and Malleson's history of the Mutiny of 1857. Get hold of that at once and also read two more books to understand human nature." These were Lavator's and Shemmelpennick's books on physiognomy.

I was extremely grateful to this venerable friend. . . . The advice did me very little direct service, but his kindness stood me in good stead. His smiling open face stayed in my memory, and I trusted his advice that Pherozeshah Mehta's acumen, memory, and ability were not essential to the making of a successful lawyer; honesty and industry were enough. And as I had a fair share of these last I felt somewhat reassured. (pt. I, ch. XXV)

Gandhi successfully brought to a close his three years of rigorous and demanding studies in England. Instead of abandoning his quest halfway through, defeated by the constant challenges or overcome by temptation and homesickness, he persisted right to the very end.

Writing about this experience makes it sound easy; but how really difficult it is to pursue studies in a foreign country where *everything* – the food, customs, traditions, and language – is different. Only when you have encountered the same circumstances in your life will you understand such difficulties.

Gandhi was able to overcome the many difficulties he encountered in England because he was honest and industrious. If you, dear reader, are honest and industrious, rest assured that everything will go well for you. If, on the contrary, you do not have these qualities, then nothing can be done. No matter what you do, you will not succeed.

XXII

The Loss of a Mother

Storms to Strengthen the Spirit

When I was returning to Japan after my first voyage abroad, I was unable to touch any food from Singapore on. Two days before arriving home I started to feel a growing excitement. I couldn't understand why I was so strongly attracted to my native country when just a year before I had left it with my mind bent on Europe.

Surely Gandhi, as he was returning to India, must have had the same sentiments as I did. His age at the time was the same as mine on my first voyage. He felt in excellent form on the stormy sea, but he writes: "The outer storm was to me a symbol of the inner." (pt. II, ch. I)

What else did he think about during his voyage? What was the force that irresistibly attracted his soul back to India, his native country?

It was his mother. His mother, the incarnation of sweetness and purity, had been the person he had most painfully missed while in England, and he was dying to see her again.

At last the boat reached Bombay where his older brother had come to greet him. With tears in their eyes the two embraced, rejoicing to see one another again.

But to his questioning about his mother there was no answer.

His mother had been dead for a long time!

> My brother had kept me ignorant of her death, which
> took place whilst I was still in England. He wanted to
> spare me the blow in a foreign land. The news, how-
> ever, was none the less a severe shock to me. But I
> must not dwell upon it. My grief was even greater
> than over my father's death. Most of my cherished
> hopes were shattered. (pt. II, ch. I)

Suffering comes after pleasure, yang after yin, sadness to those who were joyful. This is a fundamental law of life. The sea, mounting up in fury on Gandhi's trip back to India, was a symbol of the stormy life that awaited him from that time on. Hence, the turbulent waves of life, in the form of persecution, repression, and violence, would pound him without pity until he was assassinated. In comparison with these cruel events, his difficulties in London were petty.

But, there was to be a brief moment of calm before the storm. Dr. Mehta, who had carefully watched over Gandhi in London, was a resident of Bombay. He offered Gandhi and his brother a place to stay in that city. This was the beginning of a lifelong friendship between Dr. Mehta and Gandhi. Through-out Gandhi's highly agitated life Dr. Mehta will often appear as a savior. A faithful friend is one of life's most precious gifts; he who has many such friends is a free man.

Dr. Mehta introduced a poet, Raychandbhai, to Gandhi. The general director of a society of jewelers in Bombay, Raychand-bhai also had the reputation of being a Shatavadhani (one who is able to remember or follow a hundred things at once). For amusement, Dr. Mehta urged Gandhi to test the prodigious memory of the poet. Gandhi picked a hundred words from all the European languages he knew, then asked the poet to repeat them. After listening calmly to the recitation, the poet repeated the words from beginning to end in perfect order. It is not rare to meet such a man in India.

However, Gandhi was not unduly impressed with this unusual talent. There are people who give themselves over completely to mysterious forces. They worship the person who possesses these powers as though he were God, and become his disciple. Dazzled by feats of magic and supernatural abilities, some care for nothing else. Correspondingly, there are individuals who know how to exploit this childish mentality with some skill. But Gandhi was not the simplistic and superstitious type of person who allows himself to be exploited in this manner.

Gandhi, for his part, never stopped searching for the way of Truth, for the way which is not the monopoly of only those who are fortunate enough to have a special talent. He sought a way that could be practiced by anyone, anywhere, anytime.

Raychandbhai managed a business that annually generated hundreds of thousands of rupees. In addition, from time to time he pondered over philosophy and wrote commentaries on religion, sacred texts, poetry, and prose. Frequently he conversed with Gandhi on such profound mysteries as life, infinity, and eternity. (How many young people like these two do we have today?)

What Gandhi was looking for, however, was a master who could teach him the way of Truth; for in Hinduism it is taught that without a guru one cannot attain true knowledge. He regretted not being able to find such a teacher throughout his life. He was, though, able to obtain a great deal of guidance from three sources:

> Thus, though I could not place Raychandbhai on the throne of my heart as Guru, we shall see how he was, on many occasions, my guide and helper. Three

moderns have left a deep impress on my life, and captivated me: Raychandbhai by his living contact; Tolstoy by his book, *The Kingdom of God is Within You*; and Ruskin by his *Unto This Last*. (pt. II, ch. I)

But Gandhi had something that more than made up for his lack of a guru: *the attitude of infinite striving for perfection*. It was this guiding principle that enabled him to make steady progress and to become one of the most important figures of the modern world. He felt that he must always strive to improve himself, that he must continually forge ahead. This persistent progress until the very end is what is called in Japanese "Syozin," or the development of judgment. Without a vegetarian diet it is impossible.

During his childhood, from the biological and physiological standpoint, Gandhi had discovered the way of vegetarianism. It was precisely because of vegetarianism that he was able to maintain his monumental striving for Infinity until the last moment of his life.

Compelled by poverty, and without knowing its value, I more or less followed the vegetarian way from birth to the end of infancy. Later, at the age of twenty, I discovered the superiority of the vegetarian regime, and for the past forty years I have been following it and teaching it to others.

Through this experience I have come to the conclusion that the vegetarian diet should not be uniform for all people. On the contrary, it should vary widely in keeping with the climate and ethnic traditions of each country, as well as with the physical constitution, age, and sex of the individual.

In other ages, people usually remained in their home territories without large-scale changes of residence. Thus, they were content with the simple vegetarian diet appropriate to the terrain and climate that had been established as a tradition by their ancestors.

Nowadays we are living in a radically different age, one in which a capitalist, industrial, international economy prevails. Even if we remain in our ancestral country in the place where we were born, the conditions of life in that place are fundamentally different from those of the past.

As a consequence it is imperative that we establish new dietary principles for a new century of humanity. It is my task to promote this establishment.

XXIII

Justice Does Not Prevail

The First Defeat of Life

After spending some time in Bombay, Gandhi returned to his native town, Rajkot, accompanied by his brother. In order to appease the anger of those caste members who were still upset over Gandhi's trip to England, his brother bathed him in the sacred river at Nasik before they arrived home. And in order to placate them still further, his brother invited the caste to a banquet as soon as he and Gandhi arrived in town.

According to the caste rules of excommunication, none of Gandhi's relatives, including his father-in-law and mother-in-law, or even his sister and brother-in-law, had the right to receive him, even to offer him a glass of water. Respecting the will of the caste, Gandhi did not touch even a drop of water while visiting these relatives. It was at this time that his philosophy of non-resistance began to materialize.

> The result of my scrupulous conduct was that I never had occasion to be troubled by the caste; nay, I have experienced nothing but affection and generosity from the general body of the section that still regards me as excommunicated. They have even helped me in my work, without ever expecting me to do anything for the caste. It is my conviction that all these good things

105

are due to my non-resistance. Had I agitated for being admitted to the caste, had I attempted to divide it into more camps, had I provoked the castemen, they would surely have retaliated, and instead of steering clear of the storm, I should, on arrival from England, have found myself in a whirlpool of agitation, and perhaps a party to dissimulation. (pt. II, ch. II)

As was often the case, Gandhi's relationship with his wife was far from ideal. One day he went so far as to send her to live with her father, not consenting to open the door to her again until he had made her thoroughly miserable. He writes: "I saw later that all this was pure folly on my part." (pt. II, ch. II)

Finding little opportunity to gain his livelihood as a lawyer in his home town, Gandhi returned to Bombay to try to establish himself. He lasted only six months. His profession didn't go any better there, either. Thus the first chapter in the professional life of this graduate in law ended in defeat. Once again he returned to Rajkot where he opened his own office for the publication of petitions and memoranda. Thanks to help from his brother and others, this time his business went fairly well.

Even so, another big setback awaited him. This time the reversal was so serious that he was forced to leave the country. The cause of it was a clash with a British political agent. His brother had been accused of giving unsound advice to a high official whom he had been serving as secretary and counselor. The case had then gone up to the British agent who was biased against Gandhi's brother. Gandhi was at first very reluctant to exert his influence in the case, but, having known the agent in England, he went to his office to put in a good word for his brother.

Somewhat contrary to Gandhi's expectations, the agent, after listening to him for a while, said in a cutting tone: "That's enough, you must go now." Calmly, Gandhi continued to present his case. Now furious, the agent called his servant and had Gandhi thrown out bodily. This all happened within a few minutes.

At once, Gandhi drew up and sent off a note that said:

> "You have insulted me. You have assaulted me through your peon. If you make no amends, I shall have to proceed against you."
>
> Quick came the answer through his *sowar*:
>
> "You were rude to me. I asked you to go and you would not. I had no option but to order my peon to show you the door. Even after he asked you to leave the office, you did not do so. He therefore had to use just enough force to send you out. You are at liberty to proceed as you wish." (pt. II, ch. IV)

Taken aback, Gandhi related what had happened to his brother. By chance, Dr. Mehta happened to be in Rajkot at this time. Through an intermediary Gandhi asked him for advice, and got the following response:

> "Tell Gandhi," he said, "such things are the common experience of many . . . barristers. . . . He does not know British officers. . . . Let him pocket the insult. He will gain nothing by proceeding against the *sahib*, and on the contrary will very likely ruin himself." (pt. II, ch. IV)

Thus it was that Gandhi was forced to leave his native region. Because almost all legal matters passed through the office of the British agent, there was no longer a future for Gandhi there. Moreover he had now become more fully aware of the political meanness and pettiness that surrounded him, and he wanted to get away from it.

Accordingly, he left his native India, where the Englishman's word was law, and boarded a ship for South Africa where he was to take a position as an advisor for a commercial company. The salary, 105 pounds plus travel expenses, was not commensurate with the legal work he was expected to do; but he accepted the position, judging it to be the best solution to the problems mounting up around him.

However, what awaited him in South Africa was worse than the fearsome administration of the British agents in India.

XXIV

Coolie Lawyer

Aggression on a First-Class Train

Gandhi arrived in Durban, South Africa, five thousand miles from home. From the very beginning the young lawyer met opposition there, too.

One day, in the course of the week that he stayed in Durban, he visited the Tribunal. There, because he was sitting in a chair reserved for lawyers, the magistrate insisted that he remove his turban. Gandhi refused, arguing that the turban was a part of the Hindu ceremonial dress. He was then asked to leave the court.

Although Gandhi still thought of himself as the English-style gentleman that he had been in London, in South Africa all Hindus were considered "coolies." And how could the words of a "coolie" be heard before the Tribunal? From that time on he became known as the "coolie lawyer."

In a very unhappy state of mind, Gandhi departed on the first-class train for Pretoria, his final place of destination. Although the owner of his company had recommended that he reserve a sleeping berth, Gandhi, judging a first-class seat to be fully sufficient, declined to do so. At about nine o'clock that night an inspector entered his compartment and said to him:

"Come along, you must go to the van compartment."

109

"But I have a first class ticket," said I.

"That doesn't matter," rejoined the other. "I tell you, you must go to the van compartment."

"I tell you, I was permitted to travel in this compartment at Durban, and I insist on going on in it."

"No, you won't," said the official. "You must leave this compartment, or else I shall have to call a police constable to push you out."

"Yes, you may. I refuse to get out voluntarily." (pt. II, ch. VIII)

Then an agent of the police came in, seized Gandhi by the arm, and ejected him from the train just as it was leaving. His baggage was thrown out through the window.

Winter in Maritzburg, in the high regions of South Africa, is terribly cold. And the cold bit into Gandhi that night, for his overcoat had remained with his bags, which were being kept by the railroad authorities.

This night of suffering finally came to an end. Learning of the incident, the Hindus living in the area came to see him and tried to console him by relating their own misfortunes. Thus it began to dawn on Gandhi that the Hindus in South Africa were not even treated like human beings, let alone like gentlemen. Nevertheless, deciding to continue on to his destination, he courageously departed on the next train – this time with a reservation for a sleeping berth.

The next day another crisis arose, this time on the stagecoach that was taking Gandhi on the last leg of his journey. First, the agent informed him that his ticket was cancelled, hoping in this way to avoid seating Gandhi, a "coolie," inside the coach with the white passengers. When Gandhi protested, the agent insisted he sit topside next to the driver and Gandhi complied. Later, however, the agent decided to take a smoke outside and ordered Gandhi off the seat and on to the floor-board below him.

> The insult was more than I could bear. In fear and trembling I said to him, "It was you who seated me here, though I should have been accommodated inside. I put up with the insult. Now that you want to sit outside and smoke, you would have me sit at your feet. I will not do so, but I am prepared to sit inside."
> . . . The man came down on me and began heavily to box my ears. He seized me by the arm and tried to drag me down. I clung to the brass rails of the coachbox and was determined to keep my hold even at the risk of breaking my wristbones. . . . Some of the passengers were moved to pity and exclaimed: "Man, let him alone. Don't beat him. He is not to blame. He is right. If he can't stay there, let him come and sit with us." "No fear," cried the man, but he seemed somewhat crestfallen and stopped beating me. He let go my arm, swore at me a little more, and asking the Hottentot servant who was sitting on the other side of the coachbox to sit on the footboard, took the seat so vacated. (pt. II, ch. IX)

Thus, Gandhi narrowly escaped.

But his final destination was still far away, and already he had been the recipient of much cruel and merciless treatment. His heart torn by fury and anguish, he wondered: Would it be necessary to turn around and go back to his own country? Or should he fight to defend his rights before the Tribunal? In spite of everything, should he carry out his one-year commitment?

Now he was fully aware of his ignorance in thinking that he could find a more pleasant life five thousand miles from home.

Nevertheless, as he contemplated the vast, yellowing plains of Africa gleaming with light, he felt an unshakeable resolve growing in his heart.

XXV

Gandhi's Faith is Tested

A Broken Vow

Since the scope of this book is limited to Gandhi's childhood and youth, I will not go on to relate other superhuman efforts, the countless bruising battles he fought for freedom and justice in India and South Africa. For the rest of the story, I recommend that you read his *Autobiography*. This one book will add more to your life than any dozen others.

There is, however, an experience that Gandhi went through when he was fifty that I must report, because it spotlights and brings into relief the central strands of his make-up. The strands that made up the fabric of his life included fasting, vegetarianism, dietary vows, and belief in natural medicine as well as his devotion to the Truth and to *Ahimsa*.

After a very strenuous campaign to recruit Indian soldiers for the British Empire during World War I, whereby he had hoped to further India's independence, Gandhi became deathly ill. For weeks his life hung in the balance. In his efforts to survive this ordeal, Gandhi found that some of his most cherished ideals and beliefs – ones that had motivated him to extraordinary accomplishments throughout his life – were being subjected to a deadly serious challenge. He almost failed to pass this test.

113

In order to understand his path of action during this ordeal, it will be helpful to get a general sense of his ideas concerning sickness and its cure. From the following we can see that he had formed some very decisive attitudes on this subject:

> With the growing simplicity of my life, my dislike for medicines steadily increased. While practicing in Durban, I suffered for some time from debility and rheumatic inflammation. Dr. P. J. Mehta, who had come to see me, gave me treatment and I got well. After that, up to the time when I returned to India, I do not remember having suffered from any ailment to speak of. . . .
>
> Though I have had two serious illnesses in my life, I believe that man has little need to drug himself. Nine hundred ninety-nine cases out of a thousand can be brought round by means of a well-regulated diet, water and earth treatment and similar household remedies. He who runs to the doctor, *vaidya* or *hakim* for every little ailment, and swallows all kinds of vegetable and mineral drugs, not only curtails his life, but, by becoming the slave of his body instead of remaining the master, loses self-control, and ceases to be a man. . . . (pt. IV, ch. VII)

In his book, *Health Guide* (Navajivan Publishing House), Gandhi set forth many such ideas on how to achieve and maintain health through natural methods. Thus, not only was he a pioneer in politics, but also one in health. As will soon become apparent, for him there was no contradiction; rather, he considered personal health, diet, political expression, and spiritual condition all to be closely connected.

> I know it is argued that the soul has nothing to do with what one eats or drinks; that it is not what you

put inside from without, but what you express out-
wardly from within that matters. There is no doubt
some force in this. But rather than examine this rea-
soning, I shall content myself with merely declaring
my firm conviction that, for the seeker who would
live in fear of God and who would see Him face to
face, restraint in diet both as to quantity and quality is
as essential as restraint in thought and speech. (pt.
IV, ch. VIII)

But it is the supreme value that he placed on fasting that
most accurately expresses Gandhi's mentality. Here he achieved
a fusion of physical, social, and spiritual healing that is perfectly
unique in the modern world.

Like so many of the tactics that he was later to use in India,
this one had its beginnings in South Africa. There, because of
some wrong behavior on the part of residents at his Phoenix
Settlement, Gandhi decided that he must do penance.

So I imposed upon myself a fast for seven days and a
vow to have only one meal a day for a period of four
months and a half. . . .

My penance pained everybody, but it cleared the
atmosphere. Everyone came to realize what a terrible
thing it was to be sinful, and the bond that bound me
to the boys and girls became stronger and stronger.

A circumstance arising out of this incident compelled me, a little while after, to go into a fast for
fourteen days, the results of which exceeded my expectations. (pt. IV, ch. XXXVI)

This method of solving problems, even complex social and
political problems, through fasting, began to captivate Gandhi.
He thought it worked because once a person decisively put the
spiritual element over the physical element within himself,

everything around him had to fall into a like order. And if it could work on a small scale, why not on a large scale? Thus it happened that, while looking for a way to protest the Rowlatt Act of 1919 instituting martial law in India, one night Gandhi had a dream. In this dream he saw that there should be a general, country-wide *hartal*, a protest centered around prayer and fasting. The date was set for April 6th, 1919.

> But who knows how it all came about? The whole of India from one end to the other, towns as well as villages, observed a complete *hartal* on that day. It was a most wonderful spectacle. (pt. V, ch. XXX)

Throughout the remainder of his life Gandhi was to use fasting over and over again as his ultimate weapon: in 1932, his "fast unto death" in a British prison on behalf of just voting procedures for the untouchables; in February, 1943, a twenty-one day fast, again in prison; in August, 1947, his fast to stop the mutual slaughter of Hindus and Moslems in Calcutta; in 1948 his last fast in Delhi to do the same. In all, Gandhi spent six and one-half years of his life in prison.

In short, fasting was the lever that Gandhi used to liberate India!

Now, read the following confessions with this background material in mind, and with all your powers of self-reflection.

> I very nearly ruined my constitution during the recruiting campaign. In those days my food principally consisted of groundnut butter and lemons. I knew that it was possible to eat too much butter and injure one's health, and yet I allowed myself to do so. This gave me a slight attack of dysentery. I did not take serious notice of this, and went that evening to the Ashram, as was my wont every now and then. I

scarcely took any medicine in those days. I thought I should get well if I skipped a meal, and indeed I felt fairly free from trouble as I omitted the morning meal next day. I knew, however, that to be entirely free I must prolong my fast and, if I ate anything at all, I should have nothing but fruit juices.

There was some festival that day, and although I had told Kasturbai (my wife) that I should have nothing for my midday meal, she tempted me and I succumbed. As I was under a vow of taking no milk or milk products, she had specially prepared for me a sweet wheaten porridge with oil added to it instead of *ghi*. She had reserved too a bowlful of *mung* for me. I was fond of these things, and I readily took them, hoping that without coming to grief I should eat just enough to please Kasturbai and to satisfy my palate. But the devil had only been waiting for an opportunity. Instead of eating very little, I had my fill of the meal. This was sufficient invitation to the angel of death. Within an hour the dysentery appeared in acute form. . . .

All my friends surrounded me, deeply concerned. They were all love and attention, but they could not relieve my pain. And my obstinancy added to their helplesssness. I refused all medical aid. I would take no medicine, but preferred to suffer the penalty for my folly. So they looked on in helpless dismay. I must have had thirty or forty motions in twenty-four hours. I fasted, not taking even fruit juices in the beginning. The appetite had all gone. I thought all along that I had an iron frame, but I found that my body had now become a lump of clay. It had lost all power of resistance. Dr. Kanuga came and pleaded with me to take medicine. I declined. He offered to give me an injection.

I declined that too. My ignorance about injections in those days was quite ridiculous. I believed that an injection must be some kind of serum. Later I discovered that the injection that the doctor suggested was a vegetable substance, but the discovery was too late to be of any use. The motions still continued, leaving me completely exhausted. The exhaustion brought on a delirious fever. The friends got more nervous, and called in more doctors. But what could they do with a patient who would not listen to them?
. . . (pt. V, ch. XXVIII)

Day after day, Gandhi continued on in this condition. Friends surrounded him, showering him with love and attention. Likewise, medical advisors came by the dozens, showering him with advice. But none of the advice could be reconciled with his painfully high standards of Truth and Justice.

I had now been trying hydrotherapy which gave some relief, but it was a hard job to build up the body. The many medical advisors overwhelmed me with advice, but I could not persuade myself to take anything. Two or three suggested meat broth as a way out of the milk vow, and cited authorities from Ayurveda in support of their advice. One of them strongly recommended eggs. But for all of them I had one answer – no.

For me, the question of diet was not one to be determined on the authority of the Shastras. It was one interwoven with my course of life which is guided by principles no longer depending on outside authority. I had no desire to live at the cost of them. How could I relinquish a principle in respect of myself, when I had enforced it relentlessly in respect of my wife, children, and friends?

This protracted and first long illness in my life thus afforded me a unique opportunity to examine my principles and to test them. One night I gave myself up to despair. I felt that I was at death's door. . . .

The morning broke without death coming. But I could not get rid of the feeling that the end was near, and so I began to devote all my waking hours to listening to the *Gita* being read to me by the inmates of the Ashram. I was incapable of reading. I was hardly inclined to talk. The slightest talk meant a strain on the brain. All interest in living had ceased, as I have never liked to live for the sake of living. It was such an agony to live on in that helpless state, doing nothing, receiving the services of friends and co-workers, and watching the body slowly wearing away. (pt. V, ch. XXVIII)

As Gandhi lay there waiting to die, another doctor was brought in to take a look at him. Gandhi immediately saw "that he was a crank like myself." But at this point he was ready to try even the unorthodox treatment of this man whom he nicknamed the "Ice Doctor."

But whatever may be the merits of his discoveries, I allowed him to experiment on my body. I did not mind external treatment. The treatment consisted in the application of ice all over the body. Whilst I am unable to endorse his claim about the effect his treatment had on me, it certainly infused in me a new hope and a new energy, and the mind naturally reacted on the body. I began to have an appetite, and to have a gentle walk for five to ten minutes. He now suggested a reform in my diet. Said he: "I assure you that you will have more energy and regain your strength quicker if you take raw eggs. Eggs are as harmless as milk. They certainly cannot come under the category of meat. And do you know that all eggs are not fertilized? There are sterilized eggs on the market." I was not, however, prepared to take even the sterilized eggs. But the improvement was enough to give me interest in public activities. (pt. V, ch. XXVIII)

With the help of the "Ice Doctor," Gandhi had been snatched from death's door; but still he remained in extremely poor condition. By now Gandhi had been out of action for many weeks and he was desperate to get back into the front lines. Accordingly, yet another doctor entered upon the scene.

He said: "I cannot rebuild your body unless you take milk. If in addition you would take iron and arsenic injections, I would guarantee fully to renovate your constitution."

"You can give me the injections," I replied, "but the milk is a different question; I have a vow against it."

"What exactly is the nature of your vow?" the doctor inquired.

I told him the whole history and the reasons behind my vow, how, since I had come to know that the cow and buffalo were subjected to the process of *phooka*, I had conceived a strong disgust for milk. Moreover, I had always held that milk is not the natural diet of man. I had therefore abjured its use altogether. Kasturbai was standing near my bed listening all the time to this conversation.

"But surely you cannot have any objection to goat's milk then," she interposed.

The doctor, too, took up the strain. "If you will take goat's milk, it will be enough for me," he said. (pt. V, ch. XXIX)

At this point Gandhi caved in. In spite of his solemn oath never to use milk, and in spite of his belief that milk is not a natural food for man, he agreed to drink goat's milk so that he might get back on his feet.

> The will to live proved stronger than the devotion to truth, and for once the votary of truth compromised his sacred ideal by eagerness to take up the Satyagraha fight. The memory of this action even now rankles in my breast and fills me with remorse, and I am constantly thinking how to give up goat's milk. But I cannot yet free myself from that subtlest of temptations, the desire to serve, which still holds me.
>
> My experiments in dietetics are dear to me as a part of my researches in *Ahimsa*. They give me recreation and joy. But my use of goat's milk today troubles me not from the viewpoint of *Ahimsa* as much as from that of truth, being no less than a breach of pledge. It seems to me that I understand the ideal of truth better than that of *Ahimsa*, and my experience tells me that, if I let go my hold of truth, I shall never be able to solve the riddle of *Ahimsa*. (pt. V, ch. XXIX)

How touching are these words of regret! Remember here that Gandhi was a man who never deviated from his path, and, too, that fasting had always been his unfailing method for regaining his health.

It is a pity that Gandhi never had the time to study diet deeply and thoroughly. Had he done so, he might well have found one that, like the macrobiotic diet, would have allowed him to live abundantly, with no food of animal origin whatsoever. Thus, there would have been no conflict between his ideals and survival.

What would you, dear reader, have done in Gandhi's shoes? What if that which you with great, great difficulty had succeeded in banishing from your life, suddenly became necessary to save your life? Would you let it back in? At any rate, I would like you to read these thoughts several times again in the future. If, each time, you are struck more strongly and deeply by these words, then you are on the right path in your development.

XXVI

Supreme Judgment

Reaching the Seventh Heaven

Is it because Gandhi was a great saint that he was so widely admired? Or because his accomplishments were on such a vast scale that even those of Jesus and Buddha pale in comparison? No. The universal admiration for Gandhi rests on a much less glamorous aspect of his character: To the very end he was a man of total self-reflection. He saw, despite the praises of others, that he was absolutely insignificant and worthless.

It is curious and paradoxical, but the greatest man of this world is the one who knows that he is the biggest criminal, the most foolish and pitiful, the ugliest one of all. Admiration is all the greater and more merited if the admired person is fully aware of his own defects.

Nothing touches our hearts so much as the last words of this autobiography. From beginning to end they are full of *mea culpa*. Veritably, Gandhi's life was a life of *mea culpa*. In other words, there was absolutely no room for complacency in his life. It was impossible for him to feel superior, and hence separate, from another human being.

> Identification with everything that lives is impossible
> without self-purification; without self-purification the
> observance of the law of *Ahimsa* must remain an

123

empty dream; God can never be realized by one who is not pure of heart. Self-purification therefore must mean purification in all the walks of life. And purification being highly infectious, purification of oneself necessarily leads to the purification of one's surroundings.

But the path of self-purification is hard and steep. To attain to perfect purity one has to become absolutely passion-free in thought, speech and action; to rise above the opposing currents of love and hatred, attachment and repulsion. I know that I have not in me as yet that triple purity, in spite of constant ceaseless striving for it. That is why the world's praise fails to move me, indeed it very often stings me. To conquer the subtle passions seems to me to be harder far than the physical conquest of the world by the force of arms. Ever since my return to India I have had experiences of the dormant passions lying hidden within me. The knowledge of them has made me feel humiliated though not defeated. The experiences and experiments have sustained me and given me great joy. But I know that I have still before me a difficult path to traverse. I must reduce myself to zero. So long as a man does not of his own free will put himself last among his fellow creatures, there is no salvation for him. *Ahimsa* is the furthest limit of humility.

In bidding farewell to the reader, for the time being at any rate, I ask him to join with me in prayer to the God of Truth that He may grant me the boon of *Ahimsa* in mind, word, and deed. (Conclusion of *An Autobiography or The Story of My Experiments with Truth* by M. K. Gandhi.)

The state or rather the destination that Gandhi is describing here is the one I call Supreme Judgment. In my study of this matter I have found that, like so many organic processes, the development of judgment can be divided into seven stages: instinctual, sensorial, emotional, intellectual, social, ideological, and supreme.

Although this is a fascinating study, I cannot go into details here, except to say that after the sixth level, which is the highest way of looking at the relative world, judgment breaks loose from the relative world altogether and enters into the absolute world. In the absolute world there is no longer right or wrong, hot or cold, good or bad, light or heavy, easy or difficult, male or female. In the absolute world there is no longer yin and yang – or any version of it. Indeed, although the Orientals called it Seventh Heaven, even the most ambitious words cannot describe the realm of Supreme Judgment. Nevertheless this is the realm that Gandhi sought to enter.

The dietary method that most directly and surely causes judgment to develop in the direction of Supreme Judgment is the one I have named "macrobiotics." Once again stating it briefly, this method teaches us how to choose, combine, prepare, and eat the proper foods.

The Chinese and Indian sages who lived many thousands of years ago were the first to describe the macrobiotic way. Lao-tsu named it the "Tao." In India the Code of Manu gave flesh to its contours. Buddha in his teaching called it "Fujimon," the gate which leads to oneness.

For thousands of years the law of Fujimon, expressed in the term "Shindofuji," taught the identity and inseparability of the human, animal, and vegetable kingdoms. Then, gradually, through the course of millenia, and especially during the last two hundred years, the grand concept of Shindofuji has lost its luster. And now, in these times of industrial revolution and scientific progress, it is considered to be the figment of a vague and hazy imagination.

For the past forty years my job has been to restore this tarnished concept to its former brilliance and then to apply it to the development of human judgment as well as to the healing of all disease. Accordingly I have extensively written about judgment and disease from a variety of aspects, from scientific problems to political problems. Now, in this work on Gandhi, I have concentrated on another, slightly different theme: the effect of upbringing and childhood experiences in the development of judgment. Specifically, what is the effect of lying on our childhood dreams, which, I maintain, are a memory of Seventh Heaven or Supreme Judgment? And I have tried to furnish clues in the various ways that lying manifests itself, so that you can tell how much lying is a part of your life.

But if you find an alarmingly high degree of lying in your life, do not be dismayed, for it is simply one of the obstacles the relative world presents to us on our way to the Absolute. April Fool! Without lies our lives would be one long sleep.

I truly hope that on your way you will meet many temptations to lie and encounter conflicts that will test your honesty, so that you will be able to grow to be a great and honest man like Gandhi.

Honesty and Integrity. This is it!

In other words, don't lie.

For his entire life Gandhi tried to live without lying either in thought or action. This is only possible if you are healthy. If you are sickly, you will keep telling lies. Only those who do not lie are capable of courageous action. You must realize in your life the six conditions of health: never tired; good appetite; good, deep sleep; good memory; never angry; and quick and smart thinking. By so doing you have already contributed to the revolution of mankind.

Gandhi crossing a footbridge in Noakhali

Afterword

It is after considerable reflection that I have decided to write this "afterword." It has now been over a year since I first encountered this work. And during this time I have lived with it, turning it over and over in my hands, now and then holding it, like a precious stone, up to the light to appraise it. Slowly I chiseled out one draft of it after another.

I'm glad I took, that I was able to take, so much time with it. Thus I have been able to test out its premises and come to an honest appraisal: It is one of the two most influential books I have read in my lifetime.

The first, *Zen Macrobiotics*, also by George Ohsawa, convinced me that Nature, especially in the form of food, is the basis of our lives. The second, *Gandhi, the Eternal Youth*, has convinced me that there is something beyond Nature – something that predates and postdates Nature – that is its primary basis. It caused me to remember that when I was young there were quite a few people around who could "turn the other cheek," and it revealed to me why they were able to do so. Encroached upon physically or mentally, they could say, "If you want this world, take it, for I have another."

There have also been, as we say nowadays, some fringe benefits. Fascinated by Gandhi's story, I looked into the geography, history, culture, and politics of India, a country about which I had known almost nothing. What a spellbinding kaleidoscope India offers to the searching, curious eye! This journey I can wholeheartedly recommend to you.

In addition, I read some of the other works on Gandhi, in order to acquaint myself more fully with the details of his life, and in order to see him from the viewpoint of other writers. I have come to the conclusion that in this relatively short work Ohsawa has given us the essence of Gandhi. I believe that the reason why he was able to do this in such a short space, and in such a short time (as was his style, Ohsawa wrote this book in less than seven days), is that Gandhi does not mystify or baffle Ohsawa.

The Western observer, approaching Gandhi from a great cultural distance, seems to react to him in two diametrically opposed ways: He immediately and totally rejects Gandhi as "a half-naked fakir," as did Winston Churchill; or he interprets the degree of distance between himself and Gandhi as a degree of his own inferiority and idolizes him.

Ohsawa, coming from a culture in many ways even further removed from the West, could not look up or down at Gandhi. On the contrary, the two are very much alike in many fundamental ways: Both are Far Easterners. Each watched his country enter into the process of Westernization, and each deeply pondered a solution for the ensuing disorder that would preserve traditional cultural values. For, while both admitted that Western technology was superior, neither thought that Western culture was superior – quite the opposite. Each was unswervingly committed to a grandiose cause. For Gandhi, it was the emancipation of India; for Ohsawa, the spread of the macrobiotic diet and philosophy throughout the world.

Like Gandhi, Ohsawa was born with a frail constitution that through dint of strenuous effort he changed into a strong and robust one. Later in life, even their physical appearances became somewhat similar. They thought alike, they acted alike, they looked alike. As Ohsawa says: "I cannot tell if I am Gandhi or it is Gandhi that is me."

There is another similarity between these two – one that came about in the course of time. It wasn't too hard to see that in the last, say, five years of his life, Gandhi had been pretty well repudiated by the socialist, rationalist, materialist elements of his party, the Congress Party. He wanted a "macrobiotic" India, and they wanted "the good life."

The same holds true for Ohsawa's position in Japan. If Japan were to become the world leader in technology and industry – and it appears that this is happening – it would have to reject the vision that Ohsawa held out to it.

Consequently, it is outside of their respective countries that the ideas of these two men have the widest currency at present. Gandhi's ideas have circled the globe to emerge in country after country as nonviolent protest movements, such as Martin Luther King's civil rights movement, while Ohsawa's ideas have catalyzed the formation of macrobiotic movements in almost all the countries of the Western World, as well as in a few of the communist countries.

Have there been any refinements in the art of lying since this book was written in 1953? Yes, I would say we have made some giant strides, that we have become marvelously sophisticated in that area. And I am not the only one to think so; others maintain that we are living in the midst of an epidemic of lying. But, according to Ohsawa, not to worry! For, according to his absolutely unique viewpoint, falsehood makes life more exciting, amusing and adventurous!

There is one other facet of this work that I think deserves a few comments: What constitutes an authentic dream? At one point Ohsawa says, "So! What luminous and joyful dream do you have? If your dream is small and petty, it would be better to abandon it right now." Does that mean we should all become worldbeaters?

No! I don't think our dream need take the form of liberating whole countries, converting the world to the macrobiotic diet, or, like Martin Luther King, of liberating an entire race of people.

How about the dream, then, of picking up the pieces of our fractured lives and fashioning them into a happy, productive life, possibly even shooting for a successful marriage with reasonably happy and healthy children? That's of course the dream that billions of our ancestors for thousands of years settled for – otherwise we wouldn't be here. Would that be too small of a dream? Not anymore it isn't. Yesterday's small and commonplace dream has become today's big and ambitious one.

"But what about the rest of the world? It is in such a mess."

Well, why not reduce the unhappiness and befuddlement in the world by first removing yourself from the list of the unhappy and befuddled? Then, and only then, will you be in a position to move. By that time, though, others, inspired by your example, will be removing themselves from that list too, and you will not be burdened with taking the credit. They are the only ones that can do it anyway; it cannot be done from the outside. God's first question will not be, "What have you done to help others?" but rather, "What have you done to help yourself?" That is the way of humility.

Kenneth G. Burns
Brookline, Massachusetts
February 11, 1985

Gandhi and Ohsawa

A Comparative Chronology

1869   Gandhi born in Porbandar, India.

1882   Gandhi, age 13, Married Kasturbai Makanji.

1888   Gandhi sails for England from Bombay.

1891   Gandhi called to the bar in London. Returns to India and learns of his mother's death. Meets Raychandra.

1893   Gandhi, age 24, sails for South Africa as legal advisor for Indian firm.
Ohsawa born in Kyoto, Japan, with given name Sakurazawa Nyoichi.

1894   Gandhi organizes Natal Indian Congress.

1896   Gandhi travels to India for his family, returns to South Africa with them.

1902   Gandhi returns to India, fails to set up successful law practice. Goes back to South Africa.
Ohsawa, age 9, loses mother and begins to take care of his younger brother and sister.

1904   Gandhi, inspired by Ruskin's *Unto This Last,* founds Phoenix Settlement.

1908   Gandhi, after general strike in Johannesburg, sentenced to two months in prison. At mass meeting in Johannesburg advocates burning of registration cards. Arrested and sentenced to two months in prison.
Ohsawa, age 15, develops tuberculosis of lungs and intestines, and other conditions.

1909   Gandhi again arrested and sentenced to three months in prison.

1910   Gandhi founds Tolstoy Farm based on the ideas of Count Leo Tolstoy.

1912   *Ohsawa*, age 19, re-establishes his health using Sagen Ishizuka's diet. Graduates from commercial high school. Attends Kobe French School.

1913   Gandhi leads march of 2000 coal miners and plantation workers to protest the treatment of Indians in South Africa. Sentenced to nine months in prison with hard labor.

1914   Gandhi, age 45, returns to India and founds ashram near Ahmedabad.
Ohsawa, age 21, travels to Europe as ship's purser.

1917   *Ohsawa* founds Kumasawa Trading Company in textiles. Starts a movement for Japanese language reform.

1918   Gandhi leads Satyagraha campaign on behalf of Ahmedabad mill workers.

1920   *Ohsawa* brings first radio transmitter and receiver to Japan. Creates an invention to improve movie and still cameras.

1921   Gandhi presides over bonfire of foreign cloth in Bombay. Adopts the "mourning costume" he will wear to the end of his life. Mass civil disobedience begins.

1922   Gandhi, age 53, arrested and sentenced to six years in prison.

1924   Gandhi begins twenty-one-day fast for Hindu-Muslim unity.

1927   *Ohsawa* elected director of the Japanese macrobiotic association and editor of its magazine.

1928   *Ohsawa* holds first macrobiotic summer camp in Hokkaido. Publishes five volumes of *The Macrobiotic Discourse* and a biography of Ishizuka.

1929   Gandhi at Lahore Congress, calls for complete independence.

Ohsawa visits Paris via the Siberian Railway without financial support.

1930   Gandhi, age 61, breaks salt laws on the beach at Dandi. Arrested and imprisoned at Yeravda. Indian Declaration of Independence proclaimed.

Ohsawa, age 37, studies at the Sorbonne and at the Pasteur Institute. Teaches Oriental Medicine, Acupuncture, Flower Arrangement, Judo, Haiku to the French people.

1931   Gandhi attends Round Table Conference in London.

Ohsawa publishes *The Unique Principle* and *The Book of Flowers* in French.

1932   Gandhi, again in Yeravda Jail, begins a fast unto death on behalf of the untouchables.

1933   Gandhi sentenced to another year of prison. Once again fasts because he is not allowed to work for the untouchables.

1935   *Ohsawa* returns to Japan and advises Generals Arake and Iimori not to wage war against Western powers.

1937   *Ohsawa* publishes *Who Are Those Who Are Destroying Japan?* which provokes strong reaction from military leaders. Out of self-protection, becomes health consultant to the Emperor's family.

1938   *Ohsawa*, age 45, elected president of the new macrobiotic association, Shokuyo-Kai. Translates and publishes *Man the Unknown* by Alexis Carrell in Japanese.

1940   Gandhi launches limited civil disobedience campaign.

Ohsawa founds Unique Principle Institute in Ohtsu.

1941   *Ohsawa* issues 100,000 copies of *Standing on the Front Line of the Health War*, once again provoking military leaders. Threatened with assassination. The Japanese Government bans *Who Are Those Who Are Destroying Japan?*

1942   Gandhi, after a "Quit India" resolution, leads nationwide Satyagraha campaign under slogan "Do or die." Arrested and imprisoned at Poona.
Ohsawa publishes *The New Science of Nutrition, The Phenomena of Life and the Environment,* and *A Study of Sun Tsu and Other Strategies.* Pressure from military government increases. Tortued by military police for six months.

1943   Gandhi, in captivity, begins twenty-one-day fast for just government.
Ohsawa publishes *The Last and Thus the Eternal Winner* in which he predicts that England would free India and that Gandhi would be killed.

1944   *Ohsawa* is captured trying to reach Moscow through Manchuria to ask Russia to mediate between Japan and the Western powers.

1945   *Ohsawa* is jailed under very severe conditions, the temperature often going to five degrees below zero. After three months of this, loses 80 percent of his vision and almost dies. Released in June. In July attempts a coup aided by Generals Iimori and Ujimori. Again captured, sent to prison, and sentenced to death. MacArthur commutes this sentence. In October publishes *Why Was Japan Defeated?*

1946   Gandhi sets out on a four-month walking tour of East Bengal to calm Hindu-Muslim violence.
Ohsawa starts seminars on the biological and educational revolution of humanity in Yokohama.

1947   Gandhi fasts to bring about peace between Hindus and Muslims in Calcutta.

1948   Gandhi, age 79, fasts for the last time in New Delhi to stop Hindu-Muslim violence. Assassinated on January 30th.
Ohsawa age 55, starts a macrobiotic study house in Hiyoshi, Tokyo.

1949   *Ohsawa* active in world government in various cities. Bases his approach on the idea that world peace is possible only when individuals first establish their own health.

1950   *Ohsawa* meets Norman Cousins at peace conference in Hiroshima. Translates and publishes *Meeting East and West* by F.S.C. Northrop in Japanese.

1952   *Ohsawa* publishes *An Eternal Youth, Biography of Benjamin Franklin* in Japanese and *The Book of Judo* in French.

1953   *Ohsawa*, age 60, leaves Japan for India to teach macrobiotics to the world. Writes *Gandhi, the Eternal Youth*.

1954   *Ohsawa* founds Indo-Japan Cultural Center in India.

1955   *Ohsawa* leaves India by boat for Africa to meet Schweitzer. Arrives in Lambarene in the Belgian Congo and begins teaching macrobiotics to the blacks. Contracts tropical ulcers, a fatal disease. Cures himself in ten days. After disagreement with Schweitzer, leaves Lambarene and goes to Paris.

1956   *Ohsawa* lectures day and night in Belgium, Switzerland, Germany, Sweden, Italy, and England. LIMA Company begins in Belgium. Macrobiotic stores and restaurants begin all over Europe.

1958   *Ohsawa* writes *Jack and Mitie* in French.

1959   *Ohsawa*, age 66, visits the United States for the first time. Publishes *Zen Macrobiotics* in mimeograph form in New York. Gives ten-day seminars during January, February, and March. Returns to the U.S. in July lecturing every day for two months at the first American macrobiotic summer camp on Long Island.

1961   *Ohsawa* leads second American macrobiotic summer camp, in Wurtsboro, New York.

1962   *Ohsawa* holds summer camp in France.

1963   *Ohsawa* publishes *Atomic Age* and *The Philosophy of the Far East* in French. Lectures in New York, Boston, and at Chico summer camp. His prediction that President Kennedy might be assassinated draws wide attention in the media.

1964   *Ohsawa* and his disciples succeed in an experiment in atomic transmutation on July 21st. Shortly afterwards, he lectures at Big Sur summer camp. Publishes *Cancer and the Philosophy of the Far East* in French.

1965   *Ohsawa* commences to organize a spiritual olympics in Japan. *You Are All Sanpaku* published in English. Continues to lecture throughout Europe and America.

1966   *Ohsawa*, age 73, publishes *The Book of Judgment* in English. On April 24th at 5:30 p.m. dies of what is diagnosed as a heart attack.

Selected Readings

Aihara, Cornellia – *The Calendar Cookbook,* G.O.M.F., 1979.

Aihara, Cornellia – *The Dō of Cooking,* G.O.M.F., 1982.

Aihara, Herman – *Acid and Alkaline,* 5th Edition, G.O.M.F., 1986.

Aihara, Herman – *Basic Macrobiotics,* Japan Publications, 1984.

Aihara, Herman – *Kaleidoscope,* G.O.M.F., 1986.

Ashe, Geoffrey – *Gandhi,* Stein & Day, 1969.

Fischer, Louis – *The Life of Mahatma Gandhi,* Macmillan, 1962.

Gandhi, M.K. – *Autobiography,* 2nd edition, Heinman, 1979.

Gandhi, M.K. – *An Autobiography or the Story of My Experiments with Truth,* 2nd edition. Greenleaf Books, 1983.

Gandhi, Mohandas K. – *Autobiography: The Story of My Experiments with Truth,* Dover, 1983

Gandhi, Mohandas K. – *An Autobiography,* Beacon Press, 1983.

Gandhi, Mohandas K. – *Gandhi's Autobiography,* Public Affairs Press, 1948.

Gandhi, M.K. – *The Health Guide,* The Crossing Press, 1978.

George Ohsawa Macrobiotic Foundation – *First Macrobiotic Cookbook,* G.O.M.F., 1985

Kotzsch, Ronald E. – *George Ohsawa and the Japanese Tradition,* Sorbengeist Publications, 1981.

Kotzsch, Ronald E. – *Macrobiotics: Yesterday and Today,* Japan Publications, 1985.

Ohsawa, George – *Zen Macrobiotics,* Ohsawa Foundation, 1965.

Ohsawa, George – *The Book of Judgment,* G.O.M.F., 1980.

Ohsawa, George – *Jack and Mitie,* G.O.M.F., 1981.

Ohsawa, George – *Atomic Age and the Philosophy of the Far East,* G.O.M.F., 1977.

Ohsawa, George – *The Unique Principle,* G.O.M.F., 1978.

Ohsawa, George – *Macrobiotics: The Way of Healing* (formerly *Cancer and the Philosophy of the Far East*), G.O.M.F., 1981.

Ohsawa, George – *Macrobiotics: An Invitation to Health and Happiness,* G.O.M.F., 1971.

Ohsawa, George – *Macrobiotic Guidebook for Living,* G.O.M.F., 1985.

Payne, Robert – *The Life and Death of Mahatma Gandhi,* E.P. Dutton, 1969.

Rolland, Romain – *Mahatma Gandhi,* Stock, 1924.

Sakurazawa, Nyoiti – (Ohsawa, George) and Dufty, William – *You Are All Sanpaku,* Citadel Press, 1965.

George Ohsawa wrote over 300 works in Japanese, French, and English. A complete list of books can be found in *Macrobiotics: Yesterday and Today.* All English titles are available from the George Ohsawa Macrobiotic Foundation, 1511 Robinson Street, Oroville, California 95965. (916) 533-7702.